Free the Wild Monoid!

The Strings Which Unite Computer Science and Molecular Biology

CASE STUDIES IN COMPUTER SCIENCE
VOLUME 1

> "Somebody has to do the hard jobs."
> – Mark Weaver in *The Wreck of the* Phosploion

> It must have been tough in ancient days, since they didn't have either the zero or the space.
> – James M. Waclawik

> I revert to the doctrinal methods of the thirteenth century, inspired by the general hope of getting something done.
> – G. K. Chesterton
> *Heretics*, CW1:46

> "I often stare at windows."
> – G. K. Chesterton
> "The Crime of Gabriel Gale"
> in *The Poet and the Lunatics*

...Blasphemy has been regarded as something bold and splendid, as if the very essence of blasphemy were not the commonplace. It is the very definition of profanity that it thinks and speaks of certain things prosaically, which other men think and speak of poetically. It is thus a defeat of the imagination, and a volume full of the wildest pictures and most impious jests remains in its essential character a piece of poor literalism, a humdrum affair. Murder, for instance, is quite overrated, aesthetically. I am assured by persons on whose judgment I rely, and whose experience has, presumably, been wide, that the feelings of a murderer are of a quite futile character. What could be stupider than kicking to pieces, like a child, a machine you know nothing about, the variety and ingenuity of which should keep any imaginative person watching it delightedly day and night? Say we are acquainted with such a human machine; let us say, a rich uncle. A human engine is inexhaustible in its possibilities; however long and unrewarding has been our knowledge of the avuncular machine, we never know that the very moment that we lift the assassin's knife the machine is not about to grind forth some exquisite epigram which it would make life worth living to hear, or even, by some spasm of internal clockwork, produce a cheque. To kill him is clearly prosaic. Alive, he is a miracle; dead, he is merely a débris... I have taken these two instances, as the first that come to hand, of the general fact of the mean and matter-of-fact character of the vices, the **wild and thrilling character of the virtues**.
– G. K. Chesterton, "A Sermon on Cheapness" in *The Apostle and the Wild Ducks*
(emphasis added)

For more information, visit
`http://DeBellisStellarum/CSCS/cscs.htm`

* * *

Case Studies in Computer Science

Volume	Title
0	The Problem With "Problem-Solving Skills"
1	Free the Wild Monoid! (this volume)
2	(on papally assisted file transport – in preparation)
3	Sometimes... (Habitation of Chimham Publishing Company)
4	(on primes and other numerical curiosities – in preparation)

Free the Wild Monoid!

The Strings Which Unite
Computer Science and Molecular Biology

Peter J. Floriani, Ph.D.

CASE STUDIES IN COMPUTER SCIENCE
VOLUME 1

Penn Street Productions
Reading, PA

Dedication

Ad Majorem Dei Gloriam

Και 'ο ΛΟΓΟΣ σαρξ εγενετο και εσκενωσεν εν 'ημιν.
And the WORD was made flesh and dwelt among us.

John 1:14

With special thanks to
Joe Romano, Ph.D.
Jim Waclawik, M.S.
Wes Kaplow, Ph.D.
Chris Miller, Ph.D.
Nancy Carpentier Brown
Sandra Nierzwicki-Bauer, Ph.D.
Ellen Braun-Howland, Ph.D.

In Memoriam
my parents
Samuel R. Frankel, M.S., P.E.
and my teachers, especially:
Sr. Kathryn Mary, O.S.F.
Eugene Paolini, M.S.
Samuel L. Gulden, M.S.

Portions of this work are derived from my doctoral dissertation,
Finding Substrings of Varying Uniqueness in Ribosomal RNA Data.
Copyright © 1994 by Peter J. Floriani.

Text and cover image
Copyright © 2015 by Peter J. Floriani, Ph.D.
All rights reserved.

Produced by
Penn Street Productions,
Reading, PA

ISBN-13 978-1534751439
ISBN-10 1534751432

Table of Contents

Preface iv
Series Foreword v
Foreword for This Volume vi

What *Is* a Monoid, Anyway? 1

Part I: Why Write About Strings? 4
   1. An Introduction to Strings 6
   2. A Brief Look at the Theory of Strings 17
   3. How I Learned of a Cool Wildcard Problem 27
   4. Why Are There Ambiguous Bases? 38
Part II: The Theory of Wildcard Alphabets 42
   1. Elementary Definitions 42
   2. Strings over a Wildcard Alphabet 49
   3. Wildcards for a Two-character Base Alphabet 51
   4. Wildcards for a Three-character Base Alphabet 52
   5. Wildcards for a Four-character Base Alphabet 55
   6. Wildcards for a Five-character Base Alphabet 60
Part III: Solving the Signature String Problem 63
   1. A Statement of the Problem 64
   2. The Brute-Force Solution 67
   3. The Radix-Sort Solution 69
   4. The Complete Inverted File Solution 74
Part IV: The KMP Algorithm for Wildcard Alphabets 80
   1. A Statement of the Problem 81
   2. A Naive Application of KMP to Wildcard Strings 84
   3. Extending KMP to Handle Wildcard Strings 88
Part V: Some Other Case Studies 96
   1. Case Study: the "Awakening" 96
   2. Case Study: the "Micro" tool 99
   3. Case Study: Unique Strings 102
   4. Case Study: the Omniword 106

A Conclusion: When the Word is a Character 110

Appendix 1: The Codes of Molecular Biology 111
Appendix 2: Eight Bits or One Byte 113
Appendix 3: The Blumer DAWG/CIF Algorithm for Signatures 115

Bibliography 126
Index 128

PREFACE
(A Comment from a Friend of the Author)

I met Peter in 1990 at graduate school. He is a lunatic, but given our experiences together I must refrain from any further revelations – and so I will limit my comment to the following four ASCII characters:

/**/

James M. Waclawik

Series Foreword

This series of monographs is my attempt to enrich your own personal collection of previously solved problems – which is, in the end, the only "problem-solving skill" worthy of the name.

The "monograph" format is not the one usually expected in the modern academic world. People expect journal articles, or perhaps FACEBOOK postings. However, the monograph is a traditional approach to exotic topics for many disciplines: even Sherlock Holmes said (in *The Sign of the Four*) he was "guilty of several monographs." Besides, it is gratifying to explore such fascinating topics by this means, thereby aiding in the advance of Science writ large, and in the pursuit of Wisdom.

> I can imagine Sherlock Holmes remarking, in a light allusive fashion, that he himself had written a little monograph on the subject of cows' tails; with diagrams and tables solving the great traditional problem of how many cows' tails would reach the moon; a subject of extraordinary interest to moonlighters. And I can still more easily imagine him saying afterwards, having resumed the pipe and dressing-gown of Baker Street, "A remarkable little problem, Watson. In some of its features it was perhaps more singular than any you have been good enough to report. I do not think that even the Tooting Trouser-Stretching Mystery, or the singular little affair of the Radium Toothpick, offered more strange and sensational developments."
>
> GKC, *Irish Impressions* CW20

* * *

At the Ambrosian, we are constantly striving to synthesize – that is to unite – the various disparate topics and subjects of knowledge – indeed, we strive to see, and therefore to carry out all that is implicit in seeing, that most scientific phrase in the Creed: *Per quem omnia facta sunt* = "through Him all things were made."

We desire to be Christians first: followers of Jesus Christ, and therefore will arm ourselves with every possible weapon in the war we must wage until our deaths. That means we call upon science and literature, upon mathematics and philosophy, upon history, language, engineering... it is said in many ways, and shall be said in many ways, but for us, there is no such thing as a different subject, simply because we wish to say with St. Paul, we have resolved to know nothing but Jesus Christ and Him crucified. (1 Cor 2:2)

However, that does not mean we are locked into some sort of a morbid perpetual Good Friday asceticism. What it means is that we try to always be conscious of what it is we are doing. We have our Final End in mind, whether we are studying or reading or lecturing or working in a laboratory or playing a game or an instrument, or even walking across the campus. That is why our bells ring every hour: to remind us how little time is left to us.

– from the introduction to the Course Catalog of the Ambrosian University

Foreword for This Volume

Of course you may be wondering what a *monoid* is, and whether or not it would be safe to let even a tame one free to wander around. Let me assure you, the Free Monoid is quite safe, even when it is of the wild sort we shall discuss shortly. Its *contents*, however, can be a danger, or rather their *interpretation*, when such contents belong to a language understood by humans. But then that is why certain American books printed during World War II bore a very striking logo on the back of their title pages:

Just in case you can't quite read the words on the ribbon, it says:
"Books are the Weapons in the War of Ideas."[1]
Books really are dangerous, and writing them is risky. Which is just another way of saying "Somebody has to do the hard jobs."

Books, you see, are collections of words, and computer science sees words (be those words spoken or written, or even in electronic forms) are strings of characters (letters when written, phonemes when spoken).[2]

Words are a huge topic, considering that a symbol as trivial as A* (the "star-closure" of A, which we shall explain shortly) contains the text of *every* book and magazine and website and letter ever written, of anything which *could* be written. Indeed, it helps one understand that mystical bit in the last verse (21:25) of St. John's gospel about books filling the κοσμος. This Greek word *kosmos* is usually translated *world*, but it actually means the *universe*, the whole of creation. It's

---

[1] This image is from the reverse of the title page of *Murder Before Midnight* by A. B. Cunningham; I have one or two other books of that era with the same logo. Such metaphysical aspects enter into reality far more often than may be suspected: consider, for example, this insight into the famous battle of Lepanto in 1571: "Don John was clear in his own mind as to the terms on which Islamic aggression must be fought. ... He had been given the task of fighting a total war against another system of ideas – historically, the hardest of all wars to win. ... It followed that in the ships of the Holy League blasphemy or any other kind of religious doubt, openly expressed, had to be treated as sedition. The impending battle could be won only by men who were unanimous." Beeching, *The Galleys at Lepanto*, 197.

[2] "Words!" sighed King Azaz with delight in Juster's masterwork, *The Phantom Tollbooth* – and yet his brother the Mathemagician will delight to see us treat them as "numbers."

fitting, considering John starts by speaking about the Word.

I am quite well aware this sounds like a pun. Indeed, rather than be daunted by vast and mystical aspects, I will proceed with a bit of humor. Oh yes; the subtitle reads "The Strings Which Unite Computer Science and Molecular Biology." They really do, and it is a pity that neither discipline has yet begun to realize the advantages of mutual assistance. Cardinal Newman was right about getting the disciplines to work together,[3] and it is gratifying for me to assist in even a minor way.

Speaking of minor, the topic of wildcard alphabets is a very minor one as things go in the theory which underlies computer science, and yet wildcards play an important role in the work of molecular biologists in their study of DNA and RNA sequences. This little book will try to give a little of the simpler aspects of the theory, and consider the practical issues in a few interesting algorithms.

Peter J. Floriani, Ph.D.

Things to Have on Hand

1. A computer, with some sort of compiler/interpreter and development tools, since there will be some experiments you ought to perform

2. Your choice of writing implement[4] and a notebook (I mean a real, tactile, paper one) for taking notes, for working out puzzles, and other assignments. Probably some scrap paper will also be handy.

Don't forget:

The programming examples can be found on the website:

`http://www.DeBellisStellarum/cscs/cscs.htm`

---

[3] See Newman's *The Idea of a University*, e.g. "Discourse V: Knowledge Its Own End," and elsewhere. I have myself taken advantage of concepts from biology such as "poly-A tails" and "anastomosis" in developing software for cable television.

[4] Preferably a pencil: the "magic wand" given to Milo by the Mathemagician. With it and the bag full of words given to him by King Azaz, Milo fought the terrible Demons of Ignorance. Yes, I am again referring to Juster's *The Phantom Tollbooth*, but lest you think that "bag of words" is imaginary, in computer science it is quite real, and we call it A*. You will hear more about that shortly.

Twenty-Seven Keys

Ah, audacious enterprise,
Bringing to all avid eyes
Characters set down in print,
Dark or light or any tint

Every thought or word or deed
Found to fill the author's need
Gets inscribed in vivid prose,
Heavy logic, verse that flows,

Intimate the love, the hate,
Juries ponder, choose a fate;
Killings, terror, birth and death,
Laughter till you're out of breath.

Mighty strength books hold in store,
No less bombs in idea's war.
Oh, mighty one, riding strong
Pen in hand unsheathed in song:

Quit the quiet of your lair,
Rouse the weary, rend the air;
Sound your symbols, black on white,
Truth and thought through day and night,

Until all the earth will sing,
Virtues from our weakness bring.
We now sing with harp in tune,
Xylophone, flute, and bassoon:

Yes, we'll seek till we are dead
Zeal for books unwrote, unread.

Peter J. Floriani
made May 9, 1991

WHAT *IS* A MONOID, ANYWAY?

(Please note: you can skip this part if you already know what a monoid is.)

Hold on, Doctor. Before you begin, you gotta tell us: what's this "monoid" thing you're talking about? And what are the wild kind, and why should they be free?

Yeah, I thought that might get your curiosity cranking. But it involves a rather shadowy corner of algebra which you have probably never visited, or perhaps I should call it the basement level, where the dull and boring things, the strange, complex, and kind-of-scary things, but also the really important things are kept – just like in a real basement, where all the plumbing and wiring and heating and stuff is kept.

There's really just one tricky thing to tell you about algebra, and it's something which relatively few people ever learn, unless they study some advanced math classes, or go into computer science where this stuff comes in handy... and here it is. Don't get scared now.

There are really *lots of different kinds of algebras*.

And although that sounds really confusing, it's not. Most of us are already used to some of them, but we don't stop to think that they really are different. But let me start by giving you a non-mathematical example.

Now when you learn about language, especially when you are no longer a little kid and are reasonably grown up (say in high school) the first thing you hear is stuff like "in this language the person, number, and tense of a verb are indicated by endings." Granted you might be confused a little, and then you have to go and memorize those endings for however many conjugations there are! But *at least you already know there's such a thing as a verb.*

But when you're taking mathematics and algebra, you probably don't pay a lot of attention to that simple little idea called "addition" and stop to think about what it is... the way you think of "sing, sings, singing, sang, sung" or "eat, eats, eating, ate, eaten" or "chortle, chortles, chortling, chortled" are verbs.

In order to see the idea (and so I can get to the explanation you want) I need to explain what is going on.

Algebra, that is the common everyday sort of algebra which provides the machinery for the everyday kind of addition we use at the cash register or in our checkbooks, requires two ideas, which we'll the Set S and the operator $\oplus$. These two things form what is called an *algebraic structure*, which we write using those nifty little angle-brackets:

$< S, \oplus >$

(No, I am not ignoring you! If you want to know what a monoid is, I need to show you that. Please be patient, and let me explain these things, which are not very hard to grasp. Don't worry, there won't be a quiz.)

The Set S

First, there must be a *set of things*, which for most of the interesting cases to be examined, are going to be numbers. There are two main kinds of set which most people use when they work with numbers: the set of *whole numbers*, and the set of *real numbers*, which sometimes people simplify by calling them fractions, or decimals, or mixed numbers. (Note. we are *not* going to talk about any of this in a rigorous and formal manner, since these are not the kinds we will be exploring in this book.)

The Operator $\oplus$

As soon as we have a set, we will want to have a way of doing things with it. To keep things simple, we'll limit ourselves to doing just one thing, and we represent that action by the operator $\oplus$. But this is so general, and opens up so many possibilities (even if you cannot bear to guess what those possibilities could be!) that we will have to impose some rules to help out. (Yes, we are getting close to your answer, please be patient.)

Closure

To start with, we will impose one simple rule on the specified action. We require that whenever we take two things from the given set S, and perform that given operator $\oplus$ on them, the result must *also* be in that set. This rule is called *closure*, and mathematicians write it like this:

For any x and $y \in S$, $(x \oplus y) \in S$

For example, if we take the set S to be the regular whole numbers (also called the integers), and let our operator $\oplus$ be the regular addition operator $+$, then whenever we take any two numbers and add them, we get another number. That means, to say it formally, "the set of integers is closed under addition."

But you have to remember: we might not be playing with the good old whole numbers, and we might not be playing with the regular sort of addition you know and love. Yes, there are other sorts, and some of them you already know; you just never noticed that they work a little differently from the regular kind. The easiest kind to tell you about quickly is what we might call clock-math. When it's ten o'clock and you tell your friends you'll meet them in three hours for lunch, all of you are able to add $10 + 3$ and get 1... oh, yeah? Yeah. But don't worry, this is yet another kind of algebra, and you are going to be surprised.

The name for an algebraic structure which is closed is a *groupoid*. But that's just the first class of such things, and there are lots of them, so let's narrow things down by adding another rule.

Associativity

The second rule is called *associativity*, which is a bit tricky. I will show it to you but I won't explain it:

For any x and y and $z \in S$, $(x \oplus y) \oplus z = x \oplus (y \oplus z)$

Even if you have forgotten what that means, associativity is a very useful rule to have around, even if it looks complex, since it helps simplify things, and you do it all the time. You know that you can add (a penny and a nickel) and a dime and get the same result as when you add a penny and (a nickel and a dime). Oh yeah, that was easy, wasn't it?

Any algebraic structure which is (1) closed and (2) has associativity, is called a *semigroup*.

And now, let us roll the drum... in moments you will learn about the monoid!

Identity Element

We will add just one further rule. We will require that there is a very special sort of element within that given set S, an element which has the property that it doesn't make any change to any other element when you use that given operator on it. We call it the *identity element*, and write it with the letter e:

For any $x \in S$, $x \oplus e = e \oplus x = x$.

Of course you already know such a thing in regular addition: it's called zero. You can add zero to a number and get that same number. You can add a number to zero and get that same number. That means *zero* is the identity for addition.

But if we are talking about multiplication, then it's a little different: you can multiply a number by one and get that same number. You can multiply a number by one and get that same number. So *one* is the identity for multiplication.

Any algebraic structure which has (1) closure, (2) associativity, and (3) an identity, is known as a *monoid*.

Hence, my dear friend and very patient reader, you now know what a monoid is – and if you continue reading, you will learn what the *free* monoid is: it is the algebraic structure by which words (not numbers!) are formed.

And then we will talk about the wild form, in which the usual letters are turned into something very unusual, and you will hear what that has to do with something as relevant today as DNA sequence analysis. Oh yes, indeed.

* * *

PART I: WHY WRITE ABOUT STRINGS?

"I have a wife, a piece of string, a pencil and a knife: what more can any man want on a honeymoon."

from a letter written by GKC during his honeymoon.
Reported in Ward, *Gilbert Keith Chesterton*, 152.

As one advances in learning, one soon discovers that every branch of science has its own powerful illumination to aid in the study of things – even common things which are already well-known to the student – and with that aid, unexpected and stunning details are revealed.

The same is true with computer science. One of the early courses studied by computer scientists is usually called "Automata Theory." In that course, which lays out the mathematics providing the theoretical foundations of computer science, the student learns that a collection of a few things, each different from each other (what math people call "a finite set of distinguishable items") is called an *alphabet*, its members are its *characters*, and sequences of those characters are called *strings*. Further classification of these strings as to the means by which they may be generated or recognized leads to larger concepts such as grammars, languages, and mathematical "machines" (automata) which can perform the tasks of generation or recognition. Thus the mathematical principles for compiler design are laid, without which no one can appreciate either the theory or the practice of programming. Such principles may also underlie *human* grammars and languages, or at least shed light on their methods. Hence if one wants to understand *reading* one ought to understand Automata Theory.

Reading, of course, is a skill utterly essential to all scholars, regardless of their fields of specialization, but there are few students outside of certain specialized disciplines who are willing to spend the time to examine its underlying truths to *this* level of intensity – yet such details are necessary when one is dealing with computers which know nothing of reading, alphabets, characters, and words. Moreover, such details will aid the fields of philology, comparative linguistics, engineering, the sciences, and even literature.[5] Like the *venae comites* which accompany the arteries in the living being,[6] the various branches of mathematics follow along the branches of the Tree of Science, and they both strengthen and are strengthened by means of that accompaniment.

You may be feeling a little itchy, worried that some very difficult mathematics is lying ahead. There is some, but it's not all that hard. If you're not into it, you can skip the parts with the equations, and if you are into it, you can skip everything else... But I'd rather you didn't. There's a lot of very interesting fun ahead, since most of the path I am charting here runs through some of the

---

[5] Few realize the extent to which mathematics underlies the verbal disciplines, or the extent to which the literary arts underlie even the hardest and most rigorously mathematical of the "hard" sciences. Some of this is suggested in my book, *A Twenty-first Century Tree of Virtues*.

[6] Just as mathematics and literature and the classics ought to underlie and enrich the intellect, so too ought the sciences. Here I take an analogy from anatomy: the *venae comites* (such a cool term, from the Latin *comito* = I accompany, *comes* = a companion) are those deep veins, sometimes in pairs, which run on each side of (thereby *accompanying*) certain arteries such as the radial, ulnar, etc. See *Gray's Anatomy* 594.

oldest and most fascinating parts of history and literature, as well as some of the most elementary. Most people know how to read; they know what the letters are, how to tell them apart, and often they know how to use them. But few people, however, stop to consider them as they are: how they *really* work, why they came to be that way, and what parts of them are the essentials:

What makes a letter **be** *a letter?*
What is the trick that makes letters into words?
And once we know these things, what do they tell us?

Clearly the tricks must be very simple, since very young children can learn how to do it. The tricks must also be profoundly powerful, as we've been using them for some five thousand years without any significant change.

The biggest problem with talking about strings and searching and that sort of thing is not that the subject is hard, or novel, or specialized. It is something easy, old, and common. But it isn't something people usually notice. That's why (well, one reason why) I like to quote Chesterton. He liked to write things like this:

> "Perhaps the weapon was too big to be noticed," said the priest, with an odd little giggle.
>
> GKC "The Three Tools of Death"
> in *The Innocence of Father Brown* CW12:227

There are real things which are too big to be noticed, and often they are the really important things. Reading is very important, and the processing of text by computers is a kind of mechanical "reading" – and this includes very serious matters such as DNA sequence analysis. In such cases, speed and accuracy matter, but also cleverness, since there are some very difficult problems waiting to be solved.

But then, as a young friend of mine said, "Somebody has to do the hard jobs."

1. An Introduction to Strings

> Have I not heard that asparagus is now lowered into the open mouth on a string?
>
> GKC, *The Apostle and the Wild Ducks*, 27
>
> ...there is nothing imaginative about eating a cutlet at the end of a string....
>
> GKC ILN Mar. 24 1906, CW27:149
>
> I don't see how you could have burgled a safe inside the tower merely by dangling at the end of a string outside it.
>
> GKC "The Tower Of Treason" in CW14:314
>
> The arrangements by which the tops of top-hats can be lifted with a string, for purposes of ventilation, would never have reached its present universal success, if there had not been one sane person in the office.
>
> GKC, "The Victorian and the Arrow" Ch. 13
> *The Return of Don Quixote*
>
> Mr. Isidor Green, professional teacher of the violin, with long stringy hair and a coat faded to bottle-green...
>
> GKC, "The Thief on Trial" in *Four Faultless Felons*

Huh? What sort of a text on computer science is *THIS*??? Are you insane, Doctor?

No; you did not pick up the wrong book. And no, I am not insane, though it may appear that way sometimes. I begin with such hilarious lines in order to awaken your sense of alertness to words and to precision of meaning.[7]

Strings, in computing, are not very thin ropes or very thick threads, of the sort used for lowering asparagus into opened mouths, or for lifting the tops of top-hats. Nor, in this context, are they musical instruments like violins, played by stringy-haired musicians. They are sequences of characters...

Oh, but I have not yet said anything about *characters*. This is one of those tricky topics, since *everyone* knows that computers work with *numbers*, but then they also know that computers do *word processing*, and e-mail, and all that. So in order to find the real beginning of our *string* we need to know more about *characters*.

A Bit About Bytes

The fundamental unit of all modern computers is the BIT, which is a hybrid word made from the phrase *B*inary dig*IT*. The bit is nothing more than a switch (or a circuit or a light) which may be either OFF or ON – or, as so many of us techs say, it is either ZERO or ONE. These days the bits (switches, circuits, or lights) are made of *transistors*, a sort of electronic "valve." Transistors are made from extremely tiny bits of odd things called *P-doped* and *N-doped* silicon. Silicon and oxygen are the most common elements of the Earth: the major components of quartz, sand, and rocks; they are "doped" by adding small amounts of other elements such as gallium or arsenic. Millions of these transistors are contained on those "chips" or integrated circuits – the things which look like rectangular centipedes inside your computer, cellphone or other electronic device. How chips are made is very fascinating; it is a story of a most intense harmonious working of a number of different sciences: atomic physics, the chemistry of some unusual metals like

---

[7] It is said, and may eventually be proven, that precision in words is a requirement for humor. Without a consistent language there could be no jokes.

indium, material science, electronics, computer science, and even photography.[8]

Now, in almost all common computers, those bits (however they are really built, or made, or implemented) are always grouped together in *eights*. This is nothing more than a convenience, and it has become a traditional one. Eight bits together are called a *byte*.[9] And now we will begin to see something about the importance of *two* for computers, since there are *two* possible values for each bit. Any bit can be either 0 or 1, which means eight bits can be anything from 00000000 to 11111111. Eight bits (or one byte) may take on any of 256 different patterns. (See Appendix 2 for the complete chart.)

I must here insist that *all* digital computers, at least any of the usual kind in most homes and even in most labs, use this arrangement, or one very similar to it.[10] There isn't any other kind of memory in computers, or in any of their associated devices, be they thumb drives or CDs or DVDs or disk drives or even those old-fashioned paper tapes or punch cards. Everything, whether it's your photographs or movies or music, your notes or stories, your e-books or e-mails or software, *everything* is stored in bytes. That means every sort of data in the computer, *regardless of how it appears to us on the front side of the screen*, is being stored as bunches of zeros and ones. (Actually the data is stored as two different voltage levels, but it's lots easier to write 0 and 1 to represent them.) No matter what others may tell you, there isn't *anything else* in there. Just zero and one, like yes and no...

> But let your speech be **yea, yea: no, no**: and that which is over and above these, is of evil. (Mt 5:37, emphasis added)

It should come as no surprise to note that we computer techs do not talk or write (or think) in zeros and ones. Every once in a while we might like to use a 3 or even a 7 or an 8. And then, besides these ten splendid digits, there are those things some of us call *letters*, which are, as we shall shortly learn, just "one set of arbitrary symbols."

The Letters

So that means we have to make some sort of agreement about how to *represent* the letters and other things. That is nothing new: we humans have been doing exactly that for the roughly 5,000 years we have been keeping written records. We turn the sounds we make with our mouths into squiggles that we carve into rocks, or blotches we make by dipping the sharp end of a bird-feather (or a brush made from animal hair) into some moistened soot from a chimney and dabbing it onto the clean-scraped skin of a sheep, lamb, or goat, or onto a sheet made from pounded-out and glued-together thin slices of a plant called "papyrus" – from which we get our word "paper." We've since concocted another way of

---

[8] That's how those immensely complex things get shrunk: the trick is done with lenses. Under the microscope they look like cities, laid out in regular blocks.

[9] In American slang, "two bits" means the coin called the "quarter" (sc. dollar) worth $0.25, so "eight bits" would be one dollar. This is coincidental, but curious.

[10] Some use different groupings for their bytes, but they are rare, and analog computers don't count. Hee hee, that's a pun. There may be some experimental machines which use very different alternatives, but I have no knowledge of any such really existing computers. Fiction and imagination, or speculative designs also do not count... but that was not a pun.

making paper, by grinding up old clothes, or certain kinds of trees, cooking it up like a porridge and then letting it dry... but for now let us consider the squiggles which have been written thereon.

The choices of *what* those squiggles look like were made about 3,000 years ago, somewhere in the Middle East, and Greece and Rome brought the symbols to the perfection upon which both you and I are presently relying. Yes, there's a reason this font is called Times ROMAN... Except for maybe a slight hesitation at J and W and U, an intellectual from two thousand years ago would feel entirely comfortable with anything we print using capital letters. They look the *same*.

In those 5,000 years, there have been other sorts of written symbols. Granted, some of these did not have any *practical* way of being arranged in a particular order, such as the hieroglyphs of ancient Egypt (which we shall hear more about shortly), or the cuneiform (wedge-writing) of Assyria, or the glyphs of Meso-America, or the pictograms of China. But very early in their existence, the Semitic letters had taken on such an "ordered" character (maybe I ought to say such an ordered *quality*) to the extent that their ordered sequence was used as a scaffolding for the arrangement of poetry. This use of the Hebrew *aleph-beth* ordering may be seen in Psalms 9-10, 34, 37, 111, 112, 145, Proverbs 31:10-31 and elsewhere. In particular, in each of the 22 eight-line stanzas of Psalm 119(118), every line begins with the corresponding Hebrew letter: it is an alphabetical acrostic poem.[11]

Even more, the arrangement of Greek letters was brought to a very high level of acceptance, so much so that children's songs were made to aid in the learning of that strange list of letters... a list they named from its first two items: the *Alpha-Beta*:

εστ' αλφα, βητα, γαμμα, δελτα τ', ει, τε, και
ζητ' ητα, θητ, ιωτα, καππα, λαμβδα, μυ,
νυ, ξει, το ου, πει, 'ρω, το σιγμα, ταυ, το υ,
παροντα φει τε, χει τε, τω ψει, εις το ω.[12]

Here's what that song looks like using the Roman alphabet, providing you pronounce the *ê* and *ô* as *long* vowels, and all the others *short*:

Est' alpha, bêta, gamma, delta, t' ei, kai
zêt', êta, thêt, iôta, kappa, lambda, mu,
nu, xei, to ou, pei, rhô, to sigma, tau, to u,
paronta phei te, chei te, tô psei, eis to ô.

Yes, that's the ancient Greek "alphabet song," and I am very sorry that I do not have the tune for it.

---

[11] See (e.g.) Jaki, *Praying the Psalms*, 207.

[12] Athenaeus, *The Sophist's Banquet*. X, 453 D, quoted in Marrou, *A History of Education in Antiquity*, 151, which says it dates from the fifth century. The tune has not yet been discovered. According to Goodwin's *Greek Grammar* §4, the pronunciation here given for ε, ο, υ, ω is that of the Athenians "of the best period." Greek grammarians used ε ψιλον (*e psilon*) = "simple e" and υ ψιλον (*u psilon*) = "simple u" for ε and υ to distinguish them from αι and οι which then had similar sounds. The two o-names refer to what we now call the "length" of the vowel: ο μικρον (*o mikron*)= "little or small o" and ω μεγα (*ô mega*) = "large or great o."

As odd as it may seem to find such things in a supposedly modern book on technical matters, it is worth considering them because they remind us of the certain essential truths about well-known things which are all too readily overlooked. Indeed, the alphabet is *very* well known, very important and quite old, at least two millennia, but at the same time it is merely an *arbitrary* arrangement:

> The alphabet is one set of arbitrary symbols. The figures of heraldry are another set of arbitrary symbols. In the fourteenth century every gentleman knew one: in the twentieth century every gentleman knows the other.[13]

Nothing, neither in nature nor in pure logic, dictates its order, or the association between the symbol and its corresponding sound. The symbols themselves and their fixed sequence are *traditional*, ordained by long-accepted convention.[14]

If you want to begin to catch on to this arbitrary thing, just consider symbols like "H" or "X" or "P":

H: The Greeks called it ητα (*êta*) and used it for their long-e sound. The Romans called it *ha*, and used it for the sound we use it for, but the Greeks called that Roman letter "*dasia*" from 'η δασεια προσωδια (*hê daseia prosôdia*) = "the hard aspiration." We call it "aitch" which is really the French *hache* = "hatchet, axe."

X: The Greeks called it χι (*chi*) which according to some wasn't pronounced the way it looks, as it is thought to have stood for a *k*-sound followed by that "hard aspiration." But the Romans used X (they called it *ix*) for the *k-s* sound, which the Greeks represented by the Ξ character. We call it "ecks." (In my corner of Pennsylvania "ecks" are scrambled (or fried) and eaten with bacon.)

P: The Greeks called it 'ρω (*rhô*) with a long o, the R trilled as in Spanish, and that hard aspiration at the start, but the Romans called it *pay*. We call it "pea." (But according to one dictionary that is not a real word, since the word "peas" that looks plural is really singular...)

There is much more to be said about these and the other letters, and you can find fascinating discussions about them in the references, but we must proceed.

In the same way, faced with the 256 possibilities of an eight-bit byte, we must rely on a *new* agreement. That agreement is known as ASCII, for the American Standard Code for Information Interchange. You can see the list of its characters in Appendix 2; for now I will just mention a few, along with their decimal equivalents:

```
0010 0000   32   space (also called blank)
0010 1110   46   period
0011 0000   48   zero
0011 0001   49   one
0100 0001   65   capital (upper case) A
0110 0001   97   small (lower case) a
```

---

[13] GKC ILN Dec. 2, 1905, CW27:70.
[14] Hence GKC's famous dictum, "Free speech is a paradox." GKC, *Browning*, "The Ring and the Book." (In other words, the only way in which one may speak or write freely is by strict obedience to the rules of langauge.)

All this, however, is merely an agreement, as I said. There are other codes which make other associations. There is nothing inherently special about 65 which makes it suitable for the capital A, though the difference of 32 between the capital and the corresponding small letter was intended, just as it was intended that the space be assigned a *smaller* value than any other printing symbol, the digits and most punctuation be smaller than the letters, the digits and the alphabet be in strictly adjacent ascending order, and the lower-case letters come *after* the capitals.

What Is the Point?

I have bothered to go into some detail about all this for the same reason that I began with some goofy Chesterton lines: in order to awaken your attention – because the characters and strings we will be playing with are *not* those typically found in common use nor even inside computers. They are mathematical objects, just as numbers are mathematical objects – and by now you ought to know that the things inside computers are *not* numbers, as much as we may speak of them that way sometimes. They are *representations*, and nothing more.

Yes, even though I made this point about representations of numbers in the previous volume of this series, I must say it again, and with somewhat greater force. The things inside computers are *representations* of other things: fixed, finite, and possible only because we have entered into an *agreement* about what those computerized things represent. You can, and in fact, I myself have several times, arranged things inside the computer to do something utterly different from what the usual meanings of letters and numbers are... no, not by getting out a soldering iron and re-arranging the circuits, but by altering the agreement about what those 256 patterns stand for out here in the Real World. It's not all that unusual; most programmers do this so often they hardly ever notice it.

This time, we are going to notice... not because we are going to explore such curious sorts of computer problems, but because we are going to explore more about this agreement and what sorts of things have to be agreed to, in order that we might be able to do some of those curious things (or even normal every-day sorts of things) on a computer. But in order to do that we are going to have to *try with both hands*.

Er... yes. That's what I said. Try with both hands.

There is a very famous phrase in *Through the Looking-Glass* where the Red Queen says to Alice: "You couldn't deny that, even if you tried with both hands."[15] In this case, we are going to affirm with both hands. Moreover, we are going to explain why *both hands* are important. It's one of those obvious things which are so large nobody ever notices it, not even most programmers who ought to be aware of such things.

---

[15] Carroll, *Through the Looking-Glass*, Chapter 9, "Queen Alice." It is important to emphasize that Lewis Carroll was the pen-name of C. L. Dodgson, a professor of mathematics; also to emphasize that the name "Alice" (the real name of the daughter of a colleague, the Dr. Liddell of the great *Greek Lexicon* known as "Liddell and Scott") comes from the Greek αληθεια (*alêtheia*) which means "truth."

The Chirality of Letters

One of my many interests is the ancient writing known as Egyptian Hieroglyphics. I've always enjoyed examining its neat little symbols and used to borrow library books on it until my father bought a copy of Gardiner's *An Egyptian Grammar* for me when I was in high school.[16] The very first lesson, §16, explains how the little pictures are arranged in vertical columns or horizontal lines, and that the text is usually read from right to left, though for special reasons it was read from left to right; upper always comes before lower. Then Gardiner gives this little detail, to provide what we now call "disambiguation":

> The signs that represent persons, animals, and birds, as well as other signs that have fronts and backs, almost always face the beginning of the inscription in which they occur, so that the direction in which this is to be read is but rarely in doubt.[17]

He goes on to show a brief text written in all four possible ways, and adds that the ancient scribes made an effort to be artistic, to arrange the images symmetrically and to avoid gaps, and also that no spaces were left between words. Let me repeat that again: *no spaces were left between words*. This was a common style for other ancient written languages, including both Greek and Latin.

We'll come back to the matter of spaces later. But for now, let us look at this idea of the arrangement of letters a little more closely. (No, I am *not* going to proceed with an introduction to ancient Egyptian.)

The ancient Greeks occasionally used a technique of writing which went from left to right, then dropped down a line and went backwards from right to left. This was called "boustrophedon," which comes from *bous* + *strophos*, ("ox" + "turn") from the movement of plowing "as the ox turns," up one furrow and down the next. Our dot-matrix printers which print both forwards and backwards do the same thing. This sort of writing could be even more confusing than usual, since 16 of the 24 capital Greek letters of classic days are symmetric along a vertical axis:

$$A \Delta H \Theta I \Lambda M \Xi O \Pi T Y \Phi X \Psi \Omega$$

They look the same coming or going. Remember, in ancient days *all* were capitals, as small letters were not invented until the Middle Ages. Hence, the ancients had to rely the eight non-symmetric letters:

$$B \Gamma E Z K N P \Sigma$$

to verify the reading direction. Just for comparison, here is how our modern letters are divided. The symmetric:

$$A H I M O T U V W X Y$$

and the non-symmetric:

$$B C D E F G J K L N P Q R S Z$$

But even if we examine languages like Hebrew or Arabic which are written from right to left, as was usual for ancient Egyptian, we can arrive at the same point – the point I brought up by the citation from Carroll about trying with both hands.

You see, in all these languages, Hebrew, Greek, Latin, Arabic, and all the tongues which rely on the Greco-Roman characters such as English or Russian, the

---

[16] I keep it within arm's reach in my reference collection, as odd as that must sound – and yet here I am referring to it in a text on computer science.
[17] Gardiner, *An Egyptian Grammar*, Lesson I, § 16.

letters may be said to have a *left* hand and a *right* hand. They are therefore *chiral*, even in cases where some of their symbols possess an axis of vertical symmetry.

This term *chiral* comes from the Greek χειρ *(cheir)* = "hand" and means "handed" as a glove is right-handed or left-handed. It is used in chemistry (especially organic and biochemistry) to describe compounds which are identical in their composition as to elements and quantities and even as to the bonds among those elements, but *not* identical as to symmetry. The discovery that such things exist followed upon the discovery of polarized light,[18] and led to the name of dextrose (from Latin *dexter* = "right") and levulose (from Latin *laevus* = "left").

But as I am now using the term, I mean that all letters of a given alphabet are chiral, not in the geometric symmetry of the symbols by which they are represented, but in a much more fundamental sense: that these letters possess strictly oriented "left-hand" and "right-hand" bonds. Hence, the letters are constrained to bind with each other in a fixed and linear manner, thus giving words an implicit direction, the singular direction which permits them to be read (and understood).[19]

We use the term *concatenate* to indicate the operation of a letter being coupled to an adjacent letter in a word as if by joining hands: we say that a string is formed by *concatenating* its characters, one after another, in a given order. The root of "concatenate" is the Latin *catena* = "chain." Letters form a word as links form a chain.

Do not be confused about the handedness I am referring to here: the point about *left* versus *right* is not with respect to a symbol like B, which clearly has a straight "left" side and a curved "right" side. I am not talking about the shapes of the letters themselves. I am talking about a deeper concept. *Every* letter (even those which have vertical symmetry like "I" or "H") has a "left" side distinct from its "right" side to ensure that it is always "read" correctly. In English, words *always* begin on the left, and proceed from left to right: the left hand of a word's left-most letter remains unjoined to any other, as does the right hand of its right-most letter. (You may disregard games such as crosswords, "Scrabble," and word-search puzzles: all these maintain true left/right chirality. That is, the left and right

---

[18] Polarized light was discovered in 1808 by the French physicist Malus; stereochemistry (the chemistry of polarizing substances) was founded by Pasteur when he separated the *stereoisomers* – the right- and left- turning forms – of tartaric acid in 1848. See *The Timetables of Science*, 258 and 316.

[19] The fact that there are palindromes – words which can be read both ways – did, noon, civic, redder, deified; Spanish *oro*, *arepera*; German *reliefpfeiler* – is a pleasant curiosity. Such things exist even in ancient tongues: Latin *esse* = to be; Greek: αιτια *(aitia)* = "cause" (Mt 19:10). Mantinband cites an example by Sidonius (back in the time before they put spaces between words):

ROMATIBISUBITOMOTIBUSIBITAMOR

which Bombaugh's *Oddities and Curiosities* gives as the second line in a couplet said to be part of a legend about St. Martin speaking to Satan. The full version is: *Signa te signa, temere me tangis et angis; Roma tibi subito motibus ibit amor*. Translated: "Cross, cross yourself; you annoy and vex me without necessity; for owing to my exertions, Rome, the object of your wishes, will soon be near." (p. 59) He also cites the famous classic

SINUMMIIMMUNIS

which might have been the advertising gimmick of a lawyer: *Si nummi immunis* = "If [you have] money, [you'll be] exempt." However, something called the "Watson-Crick palindrome" is important in molecular biology, and we will discuss those another time.

links of the word-chain remain the same even though its geometry appears displaced from strict left-to-right linearity.)

In traditional typesetting (that is, where the fonts are real things, made from metal, which you can hold in your hand) this business of joining letters was very easy to observe. Each character was placed into a wooden frame (a backbone) called a "composing stick"[20] into which the various pieces of type were stacked in preparation for printing in a printing press. But as you may still note in books printed in that way, certain groups of letters were formed as a single piece of type, usually because of the way their shapes fit together. These are called *ligatures*, and occur in the combinations f-f, f-i, f-l, f-f-i, and f-f-l.[21] I have seen others like c-t in old books, and there are two which can still be found in some digital fonts: æ for a-e and œ for o-e. Those ligatures were visible, but there are always *invisible* ligatures which bind letters into words.[22]

An easy way of visualizing my point is to let the letters be *railroad cars*, and the word or string be a train. Any given rail car may be attached to no more than *two* others: the left-hand one, which is closer to the *engine* which begins the train, and has nothing at its *left* hand, and the right-hand one, which is closer to the *caboose* which ends the train, and has nothing at its *right* hand. Of course we do permit single-letter strings (or words) where the engine and caboose are the same.

Chains of Molecules

At the risk of confusing you by appealing to something even more technical for an analogy, I will mention that this "chaining" is used by the exquisitely technical machinery of life known as deoxyribonucleic acid, DNA and ribonucleic acid, RNA. (Then again, we are going to be talking about all this at length, so we might as well begin.) As strange and mystical as it sounds, DNA is really a kind of molecular word which contains the instructions which govern life. There are just four *bases* ("letters") of DNA: A, C, G, and T, which are chemicals attached to a sugar called deoxyribose (in DNA) or ribose (in RNA). Just so you can have some sense of the size:

the bacterium (*Escherichia coli*) has	4 million bases,
yeast (*Saccharomyces cerevisiae*) has	13 million bases,
fruitfly (*Drosophila melanogaster*) has	168 million bases,
we humans (*Homo sapiens*) have around	3,000 million bases, and
corn (*Zea mays*) has around	5,000 million bases.

---

[20] See Gaskell, *A New Introduction to Bibliography*, 43-5. Anyone interested in strings, computing, or molecular biology ought to explore this old technology of printing. Indeed, there are further parallels to be noted – just for one example, consider that each piece of type always has the *reverse* shape of its actual character, just like the anti-codons of tRNA – but such things belong to another sort of study.

[21] These combinations still look "wrong" to me when I see them in modern electronically printed books, but I will forgo further comments here.

[22] It is the handling of those invisible ligatures, that is, being able to decide what constitutes a "word" in the usual sense as opposed to an arbitrary collection of characters (which includes punctuation and the space) which makes doing authentic *word* processing so tricky, and why so many so-called "search engines" are so miserable at finding anything. It also provides some fun: The editing of "chair*man*" into "chairper*son*" begs the question whether the feminine form ought to be "chairper*daughter*." I wonder how "*man*age*men*t" should be handled.

Oh yes; there are some plants which have around a hundred billion bases.[23] Yes, those are huge numbers, even applied to atoms: those 3 billion bases of DNA in our cells make a molecule which if stretched out would be over three feet long.

These long chains of bases are built by *phospodiester bonds* which link a particular carbon (called the 3′-carbon, pronounced *three-prime-carbon*) of one sugar to another particular carbon (the 5′-carbon) in the next sugar. Remember about left and right hands, or about the freight cars being coupled together? It's like that. A given RNA "word" is "read" by something called the *ribosome* in order to generate protein, and this "reading" always begins at the "starting" end, the unattached 5′-carbon, and proceeds to the 3′-carbon, the "ending" end.

Why is this idea important, that letters (and even DNA bases) are "chiral"?

It is easy enough to claim a certain "abstract" nature for an "alphabet" – the set of characters by which strings (or words) are to be constructed. Again, we do not here refer to the printed shape of the symbols. When this is done, the reading order of a given string arises from its formal association with numbers: the *first* letter of a string is associated with *one*, the *second* letter with *two*, the *third* letter with *three*, and so on, up to the n-th and last letter which is associated with whatever number that n is. The numerical association is very useful in explaining certain things about strings, in establishing their properties, in proofs about their properties and behavior, and especially in implementation within a computer. But there is something more fundamental about the left-and-right character which may shed light on other properties, especially the fact that for strings, "addition" can only occur at the free ends. That means a "string" is different in a very important way from a "number" – and that is why this strange term "monoid" comes into play, as we shall see.

There are some other ideas which we might here advance, but they are very esoteric, very strange ideas, not ideas usually proposed in this sort of introductory setting, but well worth mentioning, if only to urge some reader to deeper exploration. Having made a veritable song and dance over this left and right handedness of the usual characters of the alphabets used in human languages, and even in computer languages, the questions are obvious:

(1) What happens if the two ends of a string of such chiral characters were linked, thus forming a ring of characters, without a distinct start or end? What are such things, and are they useful?

(2) What happens if the characters had *other* sorts of "bonds" in the way the chemical elements do? For example, say the bonds worked at right angles like an L, instead of in a straight line, left-and-right. Or what if the characters had other than two bonds? (Some of this begins to sound like Egyptian hieroglyphics, which could be "fit" together so as to make a "tidy" presentation.)

We won't try to handle these questions here, but they are interesting to consider.

---

[23] See Lewin, *Genes*, 281-283 and 438; Darnell *et al.*, *Molecular Cell Biology*, 116. So much for being the dominant species on Earth! If aliens show up and want me to take them to the dominant species of the planet, I will point to the tulips in my garden and say, "They're sleeping right now. Come back in the spring."

Remember, this idea of chirality is a device to emphasize the behavior of letters – the fact that in any given word, a letter is seen as "between" two others. It is quite true that the letters may be usefully assigned ordinals as the first, second, and so on, within a given word, but the simpler notion of being "next to" another is not as readily noticed.[24] We will see more about this and other properties as we proceed into further details about letters and strings.

Space, the final frontier

There is one other topic which I want to mention at this stage. It's actually a very tricky topic, since it is as invisible as the joining between letters.

Clearly, letters are linked together to form words, and we already know that words are "joined" to form phrases or sentences or paragraphs or other components of language. We are familiar with the alphabet, and we now have some sense of the idea of the chirality of the letters, the linkage by which words are formed from letters, and the more general idea of the concatenation of characters to form a string. But as soon as we sit down at a keyboard (the typewriter kind, not the musical kind) we realize that whenever we finish typing a word we must type a "space" (also called a "blank") so as to separate one word from the next. This is not an easy thing to grasp. The ancients did not have such a thing. Here, let me show you...

---

[24] It is not directly relevant to comment on here, but I do not wish to lose the chance of jotting down one other note about this. The word for "story" in Latin is *fabula*, from which we get our word "fable." The root is a very difficult and defective verb *for* or *fari*, which means to speak, or talk. There is something about the linear character of time, that is, of history in its most formal sense, the Human Story... and this is hinted at by the strict linear nature of letters chained into words, words into sentences, sentences into stories. It is hinted at even in very simple yet deep technology as proposed in a very curious place: "Begin at the beginning. ... Go on till you reach the end: then stop." (Carroll, *Alice's Adventures in Wonderland*, ch. 12.) This is nothing more than the basic concept of programming which computer scientists call "linear flow of control."

ORATIO DOMINICA

GRAECE

AD EXEMPLUM CODICIS BIBLIORUM VATICANI
2202

ΠΑΤΕΡΗΜΩ͂Ν
ΟΕΝΤΟΙϹΟΥΡΑΝΟΙϹΑΓΙ
ΑϹΘΗΤΩΤΟΟΝΟΜΑϹΟΥ
ΕΛΘΕΤΩΗΒΑϹΙΛΕΙΑϹ·Υ
ΓΕΝΗΘΗΤΩΤΟΘΕΛΗΜΑ
ϹΟΥΩϹΕΝΟΥΡΑΝΩΚΑΙ
ΕΠΙΓΗϹ ΤΟΝΑΡΤΟΝΗ
ΜΩΝΤΟΝΕΠΙΟΥϹΙΟΝΔοϲ
ΗΜΙΝϹΗΜΕΡΟΝΚΑΙΑΦεϲ
ΗΜΙΝΤΑΟΦΕΙΛΗΜΑΤΑ
ΗΜΩΝΩϹΚΑΙΗΜΕΙϹΑΦΗ
ΚΑΜΕΝΤΟΙϹΟΦΕΙΛΕΤΑΙϲ
ΗΜΩΝΚΑΙΜΗΕΙϹΕΝΕΓ
ΚΗϹΗΜΑϹΕΙϹΠΕΙΡΑϹΜο
ΑΛΛΑΡΥϹΑΙΗΜΑϹΑΠΟΤΥ
ΠΟΝΗΡΟΥ

The above is from an amazing collection of the Lord's Prayer (a.k.a. the Our Father) printed in various languages; it shows the Greek version (in Mt 6:9-13) as it appears in the Vatican Codex of the Bible.[25]

Note in particular: ALL CAPITALS, and NO SPACES BETWEEN WORDS.

So things are different now, almost two thousand years later. Aren't they?

Well... not quite. The problem is simply that most of us are *so* used to reading that we have no idea that the space is also a character, even if we are forced to type it roughly every sixth time we press a key on our keyboard.

You see, strings are not "sentences" or "paragraphs" – they may not even be "books." But at the very least we can see... er, *we can be aware of* at least one very curious character which plays a very different role in our work, the role of formatting. Of course even paragraph breaks and italics and font-changes and the rest can be reduced to symbolic notations.[26] Such details do not concern us very much at present, but we ought to be aware that such things exist. I will say it another way, since I do want you to know about it. The characters of a given string may have different uses. They may explicitly carry a meaning, or they may somehow modify the meaning, or make that meaning more readily perceptible – that is, they may be "structural" elements, not "semantic" elements. The topic is huge and fascinating, as most of these things are... so let us now proceed to present a brief look at the theory of strings.

---

[25] Marietti, Peter. *The Lord's Prayer in 250 Languages*, 115.
[26] These things have been invented several times and given odd names like "t-roff" and "tec" (which is not how they write it, nor how they say it!) and po-script, and so on.

2. A Brief Look at the Theory of Strings

There has arisen in our time a most singular fancy: the fancy that when things go very wrong we need a practical man. It would be far truer to say, that when things go very wrong we need an unpractical man. Certainly, at least, we need a theorist. A practical man means a man accustomed to mere daily practice, to the way things commonly work. When things will not work, you must have the thinker, the man who has some doctrine about why they work at all. It is wrong to fiddle while Rome is burning; but it is quite right to study the theory of hydraulics while Rome is burning.

GKC, *What's Wrong With the World*, CW4:43

> *Amen quippe dico vobis donec transeat caelum et terra*
> *iota unum aut unus apex non praeteribit a lege donec omnia fiant.*
> "For amen I say unto you, till heaven and earth pass,
> one jot, or one tittle shall not pass of the law, till all be fulfilled."
>
> Matthew 5:18

This chapter presents a condensed and informal version of the main ideas of the theory of strings. It will come as a surprise to almost anyone outside the field, because it is comparatively simple, even if its notation is a bit unfamiliar or cumbersome, or if its proofs seem incomprehensibly dense. I will try to keep it as simple as possible without omitting anything critical. For a more rigorous presentation or further details, please consult any text on Automata Theory or Finite Algebra, which usually includes strings as an extension to the theory of the Free Monoid.

The Alphabet

As is always necessary in math, we start by declaring what we are talking about. Some 23 centuries ago Euclid did this by setting forth several axioms which he accepted without proof, since one always has to start somewhere.[27] Our alphabet is simply a finite collection (a set) of symbols which are each distinct from each other.[28] We write them as sets, and when necessary state them at the beginning of any detailed discussion.

---

[27] See his *Elements*, the foundation book of geometry, a book now over 2,000 years old and well worth exploring. This idea of basing a system on a few unproven statements is at the heart of the philosophy of science and mathematics, and is hinted at by the famous Gödel Incompleteness Theorem, but we defer this topic to another time and place. One hint we must pursue is given by GKC: "...the starting point of thought and imagination. And these, like all living things, breed from the conjunction of two, and not from one alone." *The Thing* CW3:301. This also connects to something he said in his book on Aquinas (CW2:516) but I will defer further discussion to a better time and place.

[28] For our purposes here, we will try to always choose them to be *visible*, that is, "printing" characters, though in practice the "visibility" may be something different: that is, the meaning of ASCII 32 (the "space") is to advance a fixed amount across the screen or paper without leaving any visible marks; the meaning of ASCII 13 (the "carriage return") is to return to the beginning of the current line, and the meaning of ASCII 10 (the "line feed") is to move down the screen or paper by one "line" of print. And so on.

For example:

$$A_{DNA} = \{a, c, g, t\}$$
$$A_{RNA} = \{a, c, g, u\}$$
$$A_{Digits} = \{0, 1, 2, 3, 4, 5, 6, 7, 8, 9\}$$
$$A_{English} = \{a, b, c, d, e, f, g, h, i, j, k, l, m, n, o, p, q, r, s, t, u, v, w, x, y, z\}$$
$$A_{Greek} = \{\alpha, \beta, \gamma, \delta, \varepsilon, \zeta, \eta, \theta, \iota, \kappa, \lambda, \mu, \nu, \xi, o, \pi, \rho, \sigma, \tau, \upsilon, \phi, \chi, \psi, \omega\}$$

Observe that for clarity in our examples, we choose to limit our characters to the lower-case (or small) letters.

We will often want to know how many characters our alphabet has. We denote this value, the *cardinality* of a set, by the symbol *card*(A) or by |A|.

Strings

This topic reminds me of Maria in "The Sound of Music" teaching the children to sing, but it is really that strange and mysterious trick of reading and writing which we learned so long ago we have probably forgotten about it, and moreover have never given it any thought unless we are playing a game like Scrabble, and must once again actually pay attention to how we make words.

We make words, or to be general, we make *strings*, by setting the symbols of our selected alphabet down in a series, a row or string or chain, from left to right. We use left-to-right as a convention; recall that important languages such as Hebrew and Arabic write from right to left.

The truly important idea is that the order of the selected symbols is *fixed* for that particular string: the series advances in a direct and uninterrupted manner, just as the counting integers do. This, and not mere left-to-right-ness, is the essential quality to be attained: for any given string we must know unambiguously the first character, the second, and so forth.

For example, if we are using $A_{DNA} = \{a, c, g, t\}$ and we have a string[29]

σ = tgca

then

σ_1 = t (the first character)
σ_2 = g (the second character)
σ_3 = c (the third character)
σ_4 = a (the fourth character)

Very often we will want to know how many characters are in a string, that is, its length, which we write as len(σ). So len(tgca) = 4.

---

[29] For convenience, we use lower-case Greek letters σ, τ, and so on, to refer to strings, that is, as variables or "pronouns." These symbols may then have subscripts to refer to a specific position in that string: σ_1 is the first character.

Substrings

We often need to deal with substrings: that is, contiguous portions of the character sequences within a given string. For convenience we use the following notations:

$\sigma[i \text{ to } j]$ is the $(j-i+1)$ characters of σ from i to j:

$\sigma[i \text{ to } j] = s_i \; s_{i+1} \; s_{i+2} \; ... \; s_j$

$\sigma[i \text{ for } k]$ is the k characters of σ from i to $(i+k-1)$.

$\sigma[i \text{ for } k] = s_i \; s_{i+1} \; s_{i+2} \; ... \; s_{i+k-1}$

$\sigma[i \text{ back } k]$ is the k characters of σ from $(i-k+1)$ to i.

$\sigma[i \text{ back } k] = s_{i-k+1} \; s_{i-k+2} \; s_{i-k+3} \; ... \; s_i$

Two special cases require the empty string ε which we will define shortly:

$\sigma[i \text{ for } 0] = \varepsilon$

$\sigma[i \text{ back } 0] = \varepsilon$

Also, any attempt to reference subscripts beyond the length of the given string is undefined.

Prefix and Suffix

Also for convenience, we have the following:

prefix$(\sigma, k) = \sigma[1 \text{ for } k]$

suffix$(\sigma, k) = \sigma[\text{len}(\sigma) \text{ back } k]$

Concatenation

With subscripts to represent the position of a character in a given string, we can formulate just about anything we need to do, and in fact the complete theory requires continual reference to subscripts. But since we will often need the idea of joining or *chaining together* characters and strings, we use a simpler way of representing that operation.

"Concatenation" is quite a mouthful of a word, but even as a word it has a rich heritage. The root is the Latin *catena*, which means "chain," and it also appears in the word *catenary*, which means the form of curve taken by a freely hanging chain, cable, or string. In the mathematics of computing, to concatenate means to join or chain together in adjacent fashion, as letters are set down in print.

The distinction may be made sharper by showing the difference between *adding* 2 to 3, which yields 5, and *concatenating* 2 to 3, which yields 23. In the first case, the characters signify *values*, and the operation of addition combines the values. In the second case, the characters are considered strictly as *symbols* (that is, without any further meaning): the first is simply placed adjacent to the second.[30]

The *concatenation* operator, denoted •, is simply the idea of sticking letters together to form a string (which, in common terms is a "word"). Since we know about the subscripts, we can easily write a formal way of expressing this. (Indeed, such a task is often assigned in introductory classes in string theory, so I leave this

---

[30] It's this sort of ambiguity (between the symbol and that which it signifies) which provides opportunities for humor as in the famous "Who's on first" routine of Abbott and Costello. The locus classicus is in chapter 8 of Carroll's *Through the Looking Glass*, beginning where the White Knight says "The name of the song is called HADDOCKS' EYES."

little exercise for you to tackle, or enjoy.) However, this is the sort of thing that may be introduced best by example:

Let's say our alphabet is those four famous letters, $A_{DNA} = \{\ a, c, g, t\ \}$. Then we can form 16 different strings of two characters:

a•a = aa	a•c = ac	a•g = ag	a•t = at
c•a = ca	c•c = cc	c•g = cg	c•t = ct
g•a = ga	g•c = gc	g•g = gg	g•t = gt
t•a = ta	t•c = tc	t•g = tg	t•t = tt

Or 64 strings of three characters:

aaa aac aag aat	aca acc acg act	aga agc agg agt	ata atc atg att
caa cac cag cat	cca ccc ccg cct	cga cgc cgg cgt	cta ctc ctg ctt
gaa gac gag gat	gca gcc gcg gct	gga ggc ggg ggt	gta gtc gtg gtt
taa tac tag tat	tca tcc tcg tct	tga tgc tgg tgt	tta ttc ttg ttt

And so on.

Now, this idea may seem almost absurdly simple and obvious, but that's a misleading feeling, and can be dangerous. Once one has to handle such a thing mechanically, that is, inside a computer, but even when one is doing typesetting in the old manual manner with actual chunks of metal type, one has to pay very close attention.[31] At some point, *someone* needs to consider what is really going on when these characters are stuck together.

At first it seems that concatenation (•) is just a kind of addition (+) in disguise, and there are some similarities. For example, when we concatenate a string of length *two* to a string of length *three*, we get a string of length *five*:

$$at•tac = attac$$

In fact, for any strings σ and τ over any alphabet, we have

$$len(σ•τ) = len(σ)+len(τ).$$

So there is something going on in concatenation which is like addition.

However, the most glaring difference between addition and concatenation is that the *order* in which we chain characters together makes a difference, whereas we may add numbers in any order we like. For example, we know that
$$2+3 = 5$$
and also
$$3+2 = 5.$$

---

[31] That is the meaning of that old slogan "Mind your p's and q's," since these two letters look very similar (if not identical) when one is looking at them *reversed*, as they appear in the old physical fonts. In the computer we must be careful with other things, such as the starting index of arrays (is it zero or one?) and other such trivialities. See the discussion on the famous "fencepost" error in the previous volume of this series.

But look at what happens when we concatenate:
$$2 \bullet 3 = 23$$
$$3 \bullet 2 = 32$$
To use the mathematical term, concatenation is *not commutative*.

We ought to point out that this example is almost a bit of humor, since here "23" and "32" are strings, not numbers. Please be clear on this. They *look* like numbers, and in a certain sense they *are* numbers, or would be numbers in other contexts. But in this particular example you ought to read these lines like this:

"The character 'two' concatenated to the character 'three'
 equals the string 'two, three'."

"The character 'three' concatenated to the character 'two'
 equals the string 'three, two'."

Perhaps I ought to write them this way, though this starts to look a bit like the syntax of programming languages:
$$\text{"2"} \bullet \text{"3"} = \text{"23"}$$
$$\text{"3"} \bullet \text{"2"} = \text{"32"}$$

The "idea" of things like twenty-three or thirty-two may arise when one sees them, but it ought to be staunchly suppressed in favor of seeing the distinct strings of characters.

(If all this feels like pulling apart a joke, like trying to explain "When is a door not a door? When it's a jar."... well, yes, that's exactly what I am doing. It's almost that goofy in terms of puns. And just to reassure you, I had a hard time keeping from chuckling as I typed this.)

Also, unlike addition, there isn't any subtraction in strings; there aren't any "negatives" which are also called "inverses."[32] But there *is* something like zero, which we call the "empty string" and we need to explain that next.

The Empty String

The *empty string* is usually denoted as ε, and it is the string containing no letters. Now just be careful. This thing is *not* a blank, or series of blanks, which are real but non-printing (invisible) characters. The blank, which looks like " " is merely an ASCII character, binary 0010 0000, hex 20, or decimal 32, and it has length *one*. But the string ε has length *zero*: len(ε) = 0.

This may sound like profound metaphysics, but it's just basic common sense. The empty string is an idea, symbolized by ε, just as zero is an idea symbolized by "0" or "zero." Remember we are talking about characters, and the idea of sequences of characters: the empty string is a sequence of *no* characters, so its length is zero. But a string with one space, even though it is just as "invisible" as the empty string, has length one.

In some ways ε is like *zero*, the value you start with when you're going to add up a bunch of numbers. The empty string is the value you start with when you're going to build up a bunch of letters or other characters into a string by concatenation. Mathematically speaking, the empty string ε is the *identity* for

---

[32] That is precisely why the algebraic structure is a *monoid*, not a *group*. Groups have inverses, like the negative numbers in addition. Concatenation has no *inverses* (negatives), so it's a monoid. It is *not* an Abelian monoid, because it is not *commutative*.

concatenation, just as zero is the identity for addition: when zero is added, or ε is concatenated, the original value does not change.

For any strings σ and τ over any alphabet, the following are true:

σ•ε = σ
ε•σ = σ
ε•ε = ε
σ•ε•τ = σ•τ•ε = ε•σ•τ = σ•τ

As you can see, ε behaves just like zero, since you can concatenate ε onto any string and not alter it!

Star-closure

There is one other idea from string theory we need to know about. It may be glimpsed by the very daring act of considering *all* the words one might build just by sticking letters together. It's rather like the fun of encountering a Scrabble game for the first time. It's almost daunting to consider every possible word one might make – but in theory, we need to know about them, just as mathematicians need to know about all the numbers one might need when one adds. They give that collection (which is infinite, not finite) a special name and symbol: the set of integers, **I** = { ..., –3, –2, –1, 0, 1, 2, 3, ...} And if one looks into this idea carefully, one will find that this infinite collection is really based on four simple ideas: the idea of zero, the idea of one, the idea of adding, and the idea of subtracting – and from just those four (together with the idea of induction) we have the powerful and elegant infinite collection of all whole numbers, or integers.

In a similar way, with a given alphabet A, the empty string, and concatenation, we can produce another infinite set, the set of all finite strings over that alphabet, which we call the *star-closure* (or Kleene closure), usually denoted as A*.

This concept is amazing – even frightening: A* contains *all* possible strings formed from that given alphabet. So, if the given alphabet is the one we normally use (both upper and lower case), and we add in a handful of punctuation symbols and that very handy thing called the *space* (or blank), the star-closure of that alphabet will contain *every* book, every poem, every play, every e-mail or twitter, every note or record or diary, every piece of software: everything that has ever been written or *will ever be written* – and not only that, it also contains all the various editions of those works, with every sort of typographical error, along with things which are part text, part gibberish, and things which are mere repeats of letters, and also huge, impossibly huge, mountains of sheer illegible nonsense...

It's staggering, but it's all in there. Not that A* is useful in a practical sense, since it contains an infinite number of items, but we need to know about it, just as we need to know about certain other infinite sets, like **I**, the set of the integers, or **R**, the set of the real numbers. These collections, as abstract as they are, are the treasuries upon which we computer scientists base our work, and from which we must make our selections whenever we write or compute. And when we wish to talk formally about numbers or strings, and prove theorems about them, we need such things.

These ideas – alphabet, empty string, concatenation, star-closure – form the basis of string theory. On this is built a larger realm, known as automata theory, which considers how such strings may be manipulated, recognized, generated, translated, or processed. Automata theory is the formal basis of all computing, and while all of it except for its finite branch can only be theoretical and never implemented (since its other branches require infinite objects) it is exceedingly useful and important, and it is essential for any proper understanding of computing. As fascinating and important as it is, however, we are not going to delve into it here and now – but at least I have now shown you the start of that most difficult and exciting trail.

How "Wildcards" Are Involved

You have now had a very brief introduction to the theory of characters and strings, but there's plenty more to consider. Any rigorous course on automata theory will consider the underlying properties of •, the remarkable concatenation operator. After all, those properties are what make the Free Monoid, which is the topic of this book.

As we mentioned, this • operator seems to behave like addition, and the empty string ε seems to behave like zero. However, it comes as a surprise to students, especially those who have not yet had a class in the *theory* of algebra, that there can be such things as operators which do not commute, or which lack an inverse – like the concatenation operator.[33] This peculiarity is interesting, but it is not the only peculiarity one encounters in the theory of strings. Such oddities are not merely interesting in a theoretical or abstract way, they matter when one needs to write software to deal with real-world problems.[34] They matter even more when those real-world problems demand that we extend the theory in order to treat new problems, such as those arising in molecular biology.

One interesting extension requires an alteration of the alphabet itself: the concept of a *wildcard*. The term arises in the game of poker in the sense of "deuces are wild" – that is, in playing that card game, a *two* may be deemed by its player to represent *any* other card of the deck, even one already in use, in order to produce a desired winning pattern in one's hand. The same term is in common usage by the command interpreters of operating systems, where for example the asterisk (*) may represent zero or more arbitrary characters. However, we here use the term in a formal sense, and in fact a variety of distinct wildcards will be rigorously presented – and all this work was brought about from the demands of another field of science: the work of biochemistry and molecular biology on DNA and RNA.

DNA and RNA

The investigation into these two substances, one of the deepest mysteries of biology, the study of life, began in 1869 when the Swiss physician Friedrich Miescher studied a strange precipitate from blood cells which he called *nuclein*, later called *nucleic acid*.[35] This was found to be a substance composed of carbon, hydrogen, oxygen, nitrogen, and phosphorus, and later work revealed it to be two

---

[33] The algebraic structure <A*,•, ε> for a given finite and non-empty alphabet A is formally a *monoid*, not a *group*, since concatenation (•) is closed, associative, and has an identity ε, but lacks an inverse.

[34] For example, there is a way of transforming the object <A*,•,ε> so as to provide an inverse: the Rabin-Karp transformation maps the alphabet of two characters {0, 1} to the set of 2×2 matrices of positive integers, and concatenation to matrix multiplication. (This is in my notes from graduate school, but a citation is lacking.)

[35] See Rawn, *Biochemistry*, 665 *et seq.* for this history.

very complex chemicals, deoxyribonucleic acid (DNA) and its cousin, ribonucleic acid (RNA). Subsequent investigation showed that these are *polymers*, that is, linked sequences of simpler chemicals (known as *monomers*).

DNA was found to be a sequence formed from four relatively simple organic[36] compounds called Adenine, Cytosine, Guanine, and Thymine, which are the four *bases* (A, C, G, T) of DNA. Each base is bonded to a sugar called *deoxyribose*. Each of these sugars is linked to two adjacent sugars, just like railroad cars, by a *phosphodiester bond*. RNA is just like DNA, except its sugar is *ribose*, and it uses the base called Uracil (U) instead of Thymine (T).

The chemistry of all this is fascinating, as is the entire history of this discipline – I recommend you consult any modern book on molecular biology for the details – but the amazing thing for us to note is this. In any given DNA molecule, the sequence of these four bases was neither regular nor random, but followed some particular order, and that order dictated how a given protein was to be constructed. The DNA molecule is therefore an *instruction*, to some other active instrument, just as a recipe to a cook, a musical score to a musician, or a computer program to a CPU. All such instructions specify how *something* is to be done, something unrelated to the formal character of the instruction: just as a recipe is not food, and a musical score is not the symphony, the DNA is not the protein it specifies. In the most literal sense, the DNA sequence contained INFORMATION: it was a WORD. Hence, the work of hundreds of scientists for nearly a century attests to this amazing and almost mystical observation:

> *By detailed diligent study of the chemical called DNA, one of the deepest mysteries of the living being, chemists and biologists working in harmony have discovered that* LIFE *is based upon nothing less than a* WORD *in its most literal sense: that is, an ordered and meaningful string of letters, as defined by purely abstract mathematics.*[37]

Indeed, the four bases can be seen as the four characters of the DNA alphabet, and the apparatus known to molecular biologists as the sugar-phospodiester backbone represents the concatenation of particular characters into a string.[38]

---

[36] In chemistry, *organic* compounds are those which contain carbon, as opposed to *inorganic* compounds which don't. It had once been thought that such compounds could only arise in living things (organisms) hence the term *organic*, but this was disproven in 1828 when Wöhler synthesized the organic compound urea $CO(NH_2)_2$ from inorganic substances: "Ammonium cyanate ($CNONH_4$) white solid formed by reaction of sodium cyanate and ammonium sulfate solutions is transformed to urea upon being heated at 100°C. This reaction was carried out in 1828 by Wöhler and is the first record of a so-called inorganic substance being transformed outside a living organism into a so-called organic substance." See *Van Nostrand Scientific Encyclopedia*, 334. Note: when used as a food-fad word, it is a hilarious misnomer. *All* foods are organic, except for water (H_2O), salt ($NaCl$), and baking soda ($NaHCO_3$), though none of these are truly "foods."

[37] Hence Saint John's famous words "And the WORD was made flesh" (Jn 1:14) not only reveal the great and mystical truth we celebrate at Christmas, but also declare a most technical insight about the machinery of living beings. In a lower-case but accurate sense, we (and all living things) are words made flesh.

[38] All this is most familiar to anyone who has seen or read of the old mechanical way of printing: the *type*, that is, the little chunks of lead alloy, each with its own individual letter

DNA Sequences and Ambiguities

As molecular biologists advanced in their study of DNA, they began to obtain collections of portions of the sequences from various creatures.[39] These sequences range in length from around a million for bacteria through three billion for *Homo sapiens* to over a hundred billion for some species of plants. The work of sequencing is intensely complex, though by now there are mechanical means of performing it. I will give a rough summary here, but for details please consult a molecular biology text.

A variety of chemical extractions and reactions are performed, involving the breaking out of the interesting portion of the sequence, replication of that sequence into varying lengths, and labelling: the attachment of a tracing compound, such as a radioactive isotope, to one end. Then, that collection of labelled fragments are placed in a semi-liquid (like gelatin) and subjected to *electrophoresis*: an electric current induces the fragments to move through the semi-liquid. Since all are subjected to the same current, they move by a distance which depends upon their individual weight: thus the shorter ones move further, and the longer ones not so far. Once the various fragments are spread out, the result is placed on a film, which will darken at the places where the radioactive labels are clustered. The film is developed, and the sequence can now be read.

However, as the researchers proceed with this work, they often notice that the results are ambiguous. That is, instead of a very clear indication of one base at a given position, the result plainly shows *two* or *three* or even *all four* bases present at that position. (We shall discuss why this occurs shortly.)

Now, these workers are serious professionals: they are *scientists* and thank God they are humble in the face of Reality. They most dutifully recorded this very odd fact, and it was not as if it was a comparatively rare occurrence, or merely ascribed to a "lab error." But they recorded the ambiguous cases, and chose distinct letters to stand for the various combinations of two or three or four bases. The four bases were already known by their initial letters, A, C, G, T; the six combinations of pairs are indicated by M and K, S and W, R and Y; the four combinations of triples are indicated by B, D, H, V; any of the four bases is indicated by N. The explanation for these codes derives from the chemistry of the four bases, and is given in Appendix 1.

The Wildcards of DNA

These eleven ambiguous bases or wildcards – M, K, S, W, R, Y, B, D, H, V, N – are *realities* in lab work and in the collections of genetic sequences. They are easy enough to handle when one writes software, provided one is careful about handling them – but it would be even better to understand their mathematical properties to use them correctly. We shall see a case where my assumptions about their properties resulted in an error, and also see how the matter was corrected.

---

sculptured in reverse, but with a body of exactly the same height, and a little groove on one side to permit each piece of type to fit into a form for printing. In fact, all these examples (railroad cars, pieces of lead type, DNA bases, and formal alphabets) provide mutually supporting analogies, and we shall take advantage of this as we proceed.

[39] It is only comparatively recently that the complete *genome* for various species has been obtained, but the collection is growing.

But this would have been avoided if I had made a deeper examination of the mathematical nature of wildcards.

Before we plunge into that study, I will first recount how I encountered the biological problem which demanded the manipulation of such unusual things.

3. HOW I LEARNED OF A COOL WILDCARD PROBLEM

> The worst things in man are only possible to man. At least we must confine their existence to men, unless we are prepared to admit the existence of demons. There is thus another truth in the original conception of original sin, since even in sinning man originated something. His body may have come from animals, and his soul may be torn in pieces by all sorts of doctrinal disputes and quarrels among men. But, roughly speaking, it is quite clear that he did manufacture out of the old mud or blood of material origins, with whatever mixture of more mysterious elements, a special and a mortal poison. That poison is his own recipe; it is not merely decaying animal matter. That poison is most poisonous where there are fine scientific intellects or artistic imaginations to mix it. It is just as likely to be at its best – that is, at its worst – at the end of a civilisation as at the beginning. Of this sort are all the hideous corruptions of culture; the pride, the perversions, the intellectual cruelties, the horrors of emotional exhaustion. You cannot explain that monstrous fruit by saying that our ancestors were arboreal; save, indeed, as an allegory of the Tree of Knowledge. The poison can take the form of every sort of culture – as, for instance, bacteria-culture.
>
> GKC ILN Sept 1 1928 CW34:587-8

How did I, a computer scientist, get into biology? Well, the major antecedent to my fascination was my good friend Dr. Joseph Romano, to whom I owe many thanks. I recall that I bought the Lewin book called *Genes* because of his recommendation. In 1989 when he was doing postdoctoral work at the National Institute of Health he called me to discuss a problem he had encountered in his work on the *p53* oncogene, which he was unable to solve using existing tools at that federally funded research institute.

After that discussion I determined to pursue the Ph.D., which I did in the fall of 1990. I had already obtained the M.S. in 1985 and had observed the deterioration in academics – *conspici quam prodesse*[40] was ubiquitous, and therefore I had little expectation that academics had improved in five years. In fact, things had deteriorated.

Disappointment in the Academic Exaltation of Trivia

Speaking for myself, however, being a Chestertonian, and knowing the doctrinal methods of the thirteenth century, I still had the hope of getting something done.[41] And so, as is usual for someone embarking on the doctorate, one pokes into corners, seeking for a problem, a puzzle, or a riddle which is suitable for study. This means talking with professors and reading academic journals.

Alas. The latter method was extremely disheartening. Certainly there are some very good books out there, and some very good journal articles; in fact, as you shall hear later, I found a very important journal article which gave an excellent solution to a difficult problem. And yet far too many articles in these

---

[40] Latin: *Conspici quam prodesse* = "to appear, rather than to be useful." It is the pinnacle of "self-esteem," the horrid anti-slogan of far too many businesses and academic and research institutions in the present day, more interested in their appearance than in getting things done.

[41] See GKC, *Heretics*, CW1:46: "I revert to the doctrinal methods of the thirteenth century, inspired by the general hope of getting something done."

journals, the primary vehicles for the dissemination of new discoveries by scholars all over the world, are of two kinds: childish, or boringly complex. Sometimes they present a overly brief discussion of something so theoretical and abstruse that there seems to be no reasonable way of implementing such a thing, and no way of applying it to any real-world problem; moreover the authors neither attempted an implementation, nor contemplated any application of their work. But all too often the authors spend page after page talking nebulously about something so trivial it is regularly taught in undergraduate courses in computer science... nor in all those pages did they bother to set forth any of the theory underlying their topic, nor any of the ramifications, cautions, or related matters.

This sort of pompous childishness is something other scientific fields would not tolerate. For example, no chemist would publish a paper on how to produce a liter of 1M NaOH, since it is assumed one has this skill at one's fingertips as basic lab technique. It is something which should have been learned in high school chemistry. And then, to wax eloquent over how to choose the scale, the weighing paper, and the size of the container, where to get the distilled water, or how to stand when using the scale – while paying no attention to the necessary care required in its performance due to the caustic character and particularly the deliquescence of sodium hydroxide (it can burn a hole in your skin, and it very quickly absorbs moisture from the air, hence if not handled properly it can cause injury to the experimenter, and errors may be introduced into the result)... or the underlying general method of computing molecular weight and molarity as well as the sources and ranges of error in the steps of the operation.

Real chemists don't do that... nor do they stand for otherwise intelligent *non-chemists* publishing supposedly professional papers in *chemistry* which treat of such elementary things as if it was something just discovered by those authors.

(I grant that this simple lab technique is worthy of a careful study: such things ought to exist, and be in some standard reference work. So ought the simple lab techniques of every discipline – and I think such a work would be fascinating to read – in fact I'd like a copy when it comes out! As necessary, helpful, and interesting as such things may be, to pretend that such simplistic papers rank as "scholarly research" is a bit exaggerative.)

Reading such articles was dull and tedious, and a major disappointment about my discipline and academics in general[42] – but I kept hunting.

And then, a year into the degree, sometime in mid-October of 1991, I decided I was going about my topic-search the wrong way. So I got out my campus map, checked the course catalog, and wandered over to the Biology Department.

A Huge Loose-Leaf Binder, and an Unused PC

The first floor was only labs, and I didn't see any offices. So I went up to the second floor. The first office was empty, but in the second were two professors; Dr. Sandra Nierzwicki-Bauer and Dr. Ellen Braun-Howland. There was also a personal computer sitting on one of the desks, but it was powered down; neither professor was using it. They looked up curiously as I addressed them:

---

[42] This is but a symptom of the modern academic world's failure to heed Newman's warning: "...if you drop any science out of the circle of knowledge, you cannot keep its place vacant for it; that science is forgotten; the other sciences close up, or, in other words, they exceed their proper bounds, and intrude where they have no right." Newman, *The Idea of a University*, "Discourse IV. Bearing of Other Knowledge on Theology" §2.

"Excuse me; I'm Pete Floriani, and I'm a grad student here. I'm working on my doctorate in computer science, and I'm looking for my research topic, so I was wondering if you had any problems you are working on where a computer could be helpful."

The two looked at each other with a strange look on their faces, a look I would eventually come to understand. One picked up a binder – the largest loose-leaf binder I have ever seen – and flipped it open. "We're doing _____," she stated with some professional pride, "and we use this data to do it."

(Ahem. I did not omit that phrase for security reasons. Some 20 years later I still cannot recall what it was she said: it was some very specific statement of the work they were then doing, expressed in the technical jargon of biology. However, it doesn't matter at all what she *said*, because finding out what she *meant* was my adventure, and I am about to tell you all about it.)

I certainly didn't understand what she said *then*, but I knew what questions to ask.

I stared at the huge binder. "Er – professor – you mean – that's your *data* – and you're *not* using your computer to help?" I waved a hand towards the PC.

Again they looked at each other, this time with frustration. "We asked ITS[43] and they told us they couldn't handle these kinds of files."

I was stunned. Having been in industry playing with absurdly intricate problems for more than ten years, and having done some almost incredibly crazy translations and transformations of different kinds of data, such a statement did not make sense.[44] But I was just a lowly grad student, so I said, "Do you have that data somewhere? Maybe I could get the files and see what it looks like for myself."

"It looks like this," she said, pointing to the hundreds of pages in the binder. But the other biologist found a journal article which she photocopied for me. That article gave me the necessary information on how to acquire that file for myself.

Shortly afterwards I obtained a copy of the 1991-vintage version of something called the "16S rRNA sequences" from the "Ribosomal Database Project." Excitedly I went back to my dorm holding the floppy[45] containing the file: a collection of sequences of about 1500 bases, from the rRNA component called "16S" of the cellular mechanism called the "ribosome" from 473 different species

---

[43] ITS (I forget what the initials meant) was the administrative group who ran the campus computer systems; it was *not* related to the Computer Science department. I do not recall asking the biologists if they had sought for aid from my department, but it would have been fruitless: when I convened an interdisciplinary session to discuss how computer science might assist molecular biology I presented some of the issues convered in this book and one of the CS faculty said in a bland tone, "This seems trivial and not very interesting." Then he turned to one of the biology professors and asked: "Is this important to you?" Aghast she replied, "It's my *life!*" Now, some 20 years later, apparently everyone pretends the answer will be found "on the INTERNET" presumably having evolved there. (God knows how radical a departure from Darwinistic dogma it would be to believe someone might be able to design solutions to problems!)

[44] Of course I had seen that attitude far too often in industry; it worried me to find it in academics too. Thinking back on this, I should have replied, "That's like a chemist saying he can't handle these kinds of solutions."

[45] Yes, this was in the days before thumb drives and all that. One of these floppy disks held about 1.5 megabytes.

of "prokaryotes," or bacteria.

In other words, I now had close to a megabyte of biological data, which would easily fill a fat loose-leaf binder if one printed it out – as they had.

A Simple TOOL for the Lab

Now that *I* had the data, I could arrange it in whatever manner I liked. The design choice I made is quite irrelevant; I am not in the academic community, and I shall not get a journal article out of it.[46] I proceeded as a regular professional in the industry and did the work simply and efficiently, as it was a very trivial problem, even with the relatively mediocre compiler and system I then had. Hence, in relatively short order I had built a simple little display tool which I called TOOL – a kind of RNA spreadsheet. I still have it, and it still runs without changes, so I can show you what it looks like – or see the cover for a color image:

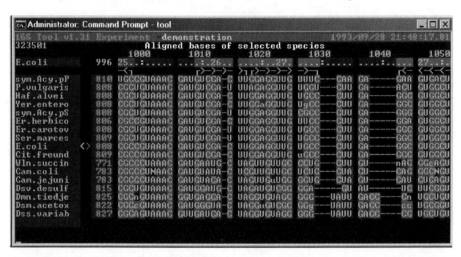

This TOOL permitted the user to select up to 16 different species – abbreviations of their names are shown in the left-hand column; note *E. coli* in the center. The program then displayed a portion of the corresponding 16S rRNA sequence, each base color-coded and aligned with the others; thus the sequences could be scrolled through and examined. The two rows at the top show the base indices of the alignment, and a secondary-structure hypothesized for *E. coli*, a well-studied species often used for reference.[47]

---

[46] It might be worth writing up as a Case Study, but the only aspect of interest would be the fact that my PC of that day was severely limited in its working (central) memory, and that constituted the major constraint on my approach. (Of course that is hardly an obstacle... so maybe it is worth writing up.) Otherwise, the interest in this topic is merely one of designing a user-interface for a relatively undefined problem, just like many of the things I did at Frankel Engineering or elsewhere; I applied the powerful technique I call "lazy evaluation" and the "doctrinal principles of the thirteenth century" – and so, as GKC said, I got things done. See the above screen shot for proof.

[47] The biologists told me that they felt it somewhat inappropriate, as *E. coli* is not a very "standard" species, but it had become the *de facto* reference species in the literature, at least as regards the primary and secondary structure of rRNA. Since that time, people have come to react to the name *E. coli* as to something dangerous, but in fact this is a benign and common species; only certain strains (varieties) are dangerous.

Since I then had no idea what these two professors were trying to do, I designed the tool in a simple and general style: it enabled the researcher to perform a few simple operations such as scrolling through the sequences, clearing the screen, displaying the nearest neighbors (by species), comparing the sequences for two species, or performing a search for a given sequence. It was a nifty little tool, considering I did it over a weekend while also dealing with teaching a class in assembly language, drinking beer, listening to rock music, Bach, and Widor, eating, sleeping, and all the usual daily business of a grad student.

When it was finished to my initial satisfaction I went back to the biologists. Again I found them in their office; again their computer was not turned on. So I asked whether they would permit me to show them something on their machine... and they did. I loaded the program and their rRNA collection, and then started it running. "So here is what I came up with..." I said, and then I explained what they were seeing.

I didn't really notice their faces, but I saw how one grabbed her clipboard and began writing feverishly.

"What... what are you writing?" I asked with concern.

"Just some ideas for things to improve."

(With some severity I kept from grinning. Ah yes, the classic response of an intelligent user; moreover, a user well on her way to being satisfied with the effort. For a moment I was back at Frankel's again, very glad to make our customer happy.)

Oh, sure it was great for the biologists. They were getting the kind of lab equipment they needed and *deserved*: equipment built by an experienced tool designer, and they had every hope that it would lead to results that would aid their work. (As it did.)

But in the computer science department, my little TOOL would have been laughed at. It had nothing impressive. It wasn't even written in "C"[48]; it had no proofs, there was no mystery about its complexity, nothing parallel or explicitly object-oriented; indeed, there was nothing challenging about it...

Or so it seemed just then.

A Broken TOOL Leads to a Wild Problem

The only aspect of the TOOL which might have been interesting to the professors was that it *had* contained an implementation of the famous linear-time Knuth-Morris-Pratt (KMP) string searching algorithm.[49] However, I was soon forced to remove that and replace it with the slower quadratic routine. But I want to tell that story in its rightful place.

Actually, the first reason the tool should have been fascinating was something I encountered in my initial examination of the 16S rRNA data.

More and more people now know that DNA uses an "alphabet" of four letters – A, C, G, T – which are the initial letters of the four "bases" or nucleotides which

---

[48] That, or rather C++, was then the popular language. It seems that most everything now being used is just a degraded (and interpretive) dialect, and the many things that should have been improved weren't. No wonder I've always felt that "C" was their grade for the project, and not its name.

[49] See e.g. Sedgewick, *Algorithms*, or any algorithms text.

make up DNA. (Note, where DNA uses T, RNA uses U.)

However, the data I had contained a few other letters: M, K, R, Y, S, W, B, D, H, V and N, as well as the hyphen, which was stuck in so as to make the various sequences align with each other. It will be instructive to see how many of these characters there were:

base	count
A	173741
C	154564
D	3
G	213084
H	8
K	6
M	26
N	7831
R	82
S	47
U	143518
V	13
W	15
Y	106

I had already known about these other letters, which are called the DNA wildcards, and because of my background in chemistry I had some understanding of what they meant, and how they were used. Because there were a significant number of them – over 8,000 wildcards in almost 700,000 total bases, or more than one percent of the data – I spent some time with the biology professors discussing them as the project advanced, and you will hear more about them shortly. Here we must simply note that these wildcards were *important*, and could *not* be ignored: they had to be dealt with properly.

Here is an example of how they work. The letter "N" may stand for any of the four bases. So when a given bacterial species has the sequence CGCnGUA, as *Desulfomonile tiedjei* str. DCB-1 does at position 999 (shown as Dmn.tiedje in the above screen shot), when a researcher searches for any of the strings CGCaGUA or CGCcGUA or CGCgGUA or CGCtGUA, *a match must be reported* at position 999 for each of these queries.

Don't worry about getting all this just now, I am going to explain it further in detail. For now, I just want to tell you what happened. One of the biologists tried to find the sequence "GTC" and the TOOL (which was then using this classic KMP search algorithm) did *not* report an appearance, even though the biologist showed me a sequence with a match... Fascinating!

I wrote down this "bug" (as usual) and looked into it. I wasn't sure what I had done wrong[50] – not immediately, anyway – but the brief answer is that this well-known Knuth-Morris-Pratt string search algorithm does *not* work when the strings or queries contain wildcards. This is a matter of some interest, and you will hear all about this later, as well as how to deal with the problem. But back then all I knew was that the famous KMP algorithm *didn't* work – so I took it out and put in the very simple (but slower) iterative search, which worked correctly.

---

[50] Unlike some people at another job I once worked for, I did not immediately blame the user.

As I said, at this early stage I didn't bother telling anyone in my department what I was doing. First of all, I needed to learn about the real project the biologists were working on, and see if what they were trying to do by hand was something I could turn into a program, so the computer could do it for them. And it would be even better if it could be turned into a doctoral project.

I came to call this project the "signature string problem," or, in a casual setting, I would say that I used the computer to find fingerprints for bacteria.[51]

Ooo, *fingerprints*. Sounds like a mystery story, doesn't it? But since this is a technical document, not a detective novel, I will tell you what was going on, rather than attempt to recount how I learned about it.

What They Wanted To Do: In-situ Hybridization

The biologists had obtained a grant (as I recall, it was from the Department of Energy) to study pollution in various environmental samples, such as mud from lakes or rivers. They hoped to use a novel technique called *in-situ hybridization* to get an estimate of *how many* and also *what kinds* of bacteria were present in a given sample. This technique would be enabled by the growing collection of known 16S rRNA of various prokaryotic (bacterial) species.

All right; that's the high-level description: that's what they wanted to do: find out the kinds of bacteria in environmental samples by doing in-situ hybridization.

Next, I need to explain how in-situ hybridization is performed. This is a lab procedure wherein one "composes" a particular RNA sequence on an instrument called a "gene synthesizer." You type in the sequence using four keys for the four bases, and the machine actually "cooks up" a tiny tube full of the *actual RNA* which has that sequence. (Yes, it's a very tiny tube, and it's an unbelievably small amount of RNA, but there's enough to do its job.) It's an astounding idea that this can be done at all... but there's more.

After the experimenters have that little tube of the desired RNA sequence, they use organic chemistry to attach a "marker" to the sequences they have just brewed. This marker can be either a radioactive marker which will then show up on film, or something which fluoresces under ultraviolet (UV) light; that was the method they used when I actually saw the thing done. The resulting substance (the RNA with an attached marker) is called the "tracer" or "probe."

Now, you take a bit of that probe (those brewed RNA sequences with attached markers) and apply it to the environmental sample, after you nudge the ribosomes to "loosen up," so that the 16S rRNA unwraps itself, and you let those marked sequences you added link together, to *hybridize*, with the 16S sequences from those cells. Whenever A pairs with U, and C pairs with G, the two (the original RNA in the ribosomes of the bacteria, and the probe with its marked and synthesized RNA) will stick together, sort of like the teeth of a zipper. And this happens thousands of times, since any given cell has tens of thousands of ribosomes.[52] But they won't stick together unless the sequences match – and that is why I say it's like their fingerprints.

---

[51] Yes, I *know* bacteria don't have fingers. And yet we can track them in almost the same way.

[52] The typical *E. coli* cell has 15,000 (or 25,000) ribosomes; a typical mammalian cell has ten million. See Rawn, *Biochemistry*, pp. 11, 853, 848.

And *then*, once the hybridization has occurred, you take that sample and put it under a microscope and shine some UV light on it, then any cells where the probe (with *your* marked sequences) has hybridized with the cellular rRNA will *light up* and hence announce their presence. You can even count them and see how many cells there are... and that gives you a clue about how many bacteria there are, and how they are doing. There it is. Very cunning.

Now, just to review, I will summarize the steps of the experiment:
1. You are given a sample from the Real World, presumably containing bacteria.
2. Select a sequence which will match those bacteria you want to know about.
3. Synthesize that sequence into RNA.[53]
4. Attach a signal, either radioactive or fluorescent. The result is your probe.
5. "Loosen up" (denature) the rRNA of the bacteria in the sample.
6. Add your probe to the sample.
7. Let the probe stick onto (hybridize with) the bacterial RNA.
8. Check the sample under UV. (Or, if using radioisotopes, by photography.)
9. That ought to reveal the presence of bacteria containing your sequence.

Now you have a basic idea of what the biologists were doing: in-situ hybridization with synthesized labelled RNA probes in order to determine and characterize prokaryotic populations.

What They Needed In Order To Do It

So, the biologists had this idea. They had the samples. They had the technique. They had all the lab tools they needed. They had a huge collection of rRNA sequence information.

But there was one *other* thing they needed – which was why they had that huge loose-leaf binder of the rRNA sequences.

They needed to figure out *which sequences* they wanted to explore.

You see, they could choose a portion of the ribosome which is common to almost all bacterial species. Or they could choose a portion which appeared to be highly variable, and which might have a portion that would be unique to a single species, or a less-variable region which could cover a group of species.

There had been studies done about what regions were "universal" across nearly all bacteria: these portions presumably play critical roles in the work of the ribosome. The biologists knew these portions – that is, some universal signatures had already been found – so they could, and did, test this method in the lab.[54]

There are other regions which were seen to be highly variable, which might serve almost like "fingerprints" for each species. The problem is to find a sequence using the rRNA collection which will accomplish the selection of those species in the actual samples by means of the above lab work. These sequences (in

---

[53] This is where you use your gene synthesizer. It's up to the individual researcher to supply the backup band. Lab coats are required.

[54] I got to see the result. Wow. It was a fascinating and curious inversion of my scientific experience to look into a *microscope* and see what looked like stars: these were the hybridized rRNA of bacteria glowing under the ultraviolet lamp. I am sorry I do not have a photograph to show you; I wish I did.

the biological sense) or strings (in the computational sense) will therefore serve as *signatures* to the various species, or to groups of species, depending on which one (or which group) contains a given sequence.

Thus, I now knew what the biologists were doing, and hence I could now understand what they meant by the forgotten _____ phrase I omitted earlier: that is, they wanted to *find suitable sequences for in-situ hybridization*. Therefore I also realized that *their* problem could be considered as a problem in my discipline, that is, in computer science.

Before we leave biology for computing and mathematics, I should mention an aspect of this in-situ hybridization technique which could bother some scientists. There are, of course, issues about sensitivity of the technique, and several other very technical matters in chemistry and biology, such as the salinity and the temperature used during hybridization. However, the important issue is this: the synthesized probe can hybridize to either DNA or RNA. Also, there is more RNA in the living cell than just the 16S rRNA, the skeletal framework of the *small* subunit of the ribosome.

In order to handle the question properly, one needs to take into account the other kinds of RNA existing in the cell: the ribosome also contains 23S and 5S rRNA, the framework of the *large* subunit. There is also messenger RNA (mRNA) and various kinds of transfer RNA (tRNA). The biologists told me they could exclude the DNA, since there was only *one* such molecule, and also any mRNA, since there were presumably relatively few of these. A typical bacterium has over ten thousand ribosomes[55] (comprised of 5S, 16S, and 23S units) which ought to provide enough to hybridize so as to be detectable by the above method. Note that this does not alter the computational problem, it only affects the data required for the intended purpose.

There is one other aspect of the biological data which is of interest to computing: it is, in fact, an aspect which makes for a very intriguing puzzle. That is, the real RNA data contains *wildcards* – symbols for ambiguous bases, and these may not be omitted nor neglected. They must be taken into account in the finding of suitable signatures.

Even more curiously, the proposed signatures could themselves contain wildcards if necessary, though the biologists preferred to avoid them. This can be done by synthesizing the various explicit sequences represented by the wildcards: for example, if the signature was GGGMTTT, they would make the probe by synthesizing both GGGaTTT and GGGcTTT.

As noted earlier, the wildcards must emphatically *not* be treated casually, as if they were just any normal character. As we shall see in Part II, they have unusual properties: the concept of "matching" is not identical with the "equality" used for normal characters and strings.

---

[55] Rawn's *Biochemistry* gives two different values for *E. coli*: 15,000 (p. 11) and 25,000 "in an actively growing" cell (p. 853). Just in case you are wondering what the S means, it represents "Svedbergs," a unit of sedimentation, which corresponds to weight. The 5S unit contains about 120 bases, the 16S about 1500, and the 23S about 2900. See *ibid.*, 849-50.

The Signature String Problem

So now I knew what the biologists were doing, and what they needed in order to do it – and I could actually see that there was a well-defined problem, and clearly one which could be handled by computers. (Ah! How grand it felt to finally have such a thing!) I came to call this problem (or family of problems) the "signature string problem," which I will now state formally, since we are now in computer science, and may therefore generalize from the particular details of molecular biology.

We are given an alphabet A and a set of *sufficiently distinct*[56] non-empty strings over that alphabet: R = $\{\rho_i\}$ with $\rho_i \in A^* - \varepsilon$. We consider three different classes of the problem, subdivided as two distinct cases indicated by the relation (equals/*matches*), which depends on the kind of data being considered: whether the alphabet is of the ordinary kind, or it contains wildcards.

1. The *individual signatures* problem:
   For each string ρ_i in R find the set $S(\rho_i)$ such that

   $S(\rho_i) = \{\sigma \mid \sigma$ (equals/*matches*) a substring of ρ_i
   but *not* any string in R–$\{\rho_i\}$. $\}$

2. The *group signatures* problem:
   Given a "group" G, a proper subset of R (G $\subset$ R), find the set S(G) such that

   $S(G) = \{\sigma \mid \sigma$ (equals/*matches*) a substring of ρ_i
   for *every* $\rho_i \in$ G but *not* any string in R–G. $\}$

3. The *universal signatures* problem:
   Given the set R, find the set S(R) such that

   $S(R) = \{\sigma \mid \sigma$ (equals/*matches*) a substring of *every* string in R. $\}$

"*Calculatus Eliminatus*": Computational *Hapax Legomena* for Molecular Biology

Now, the typical "search" algorithm in computing presumes there are *two* inputs supplied to the problem: ordinarily you know (1) what the collection is wherein you are looking, and you also know (2) a query, the thing you are searching for. However, in this case we do *not* know our query; we only know something about it. We know it must appear in the RNA of certain species, and must *not* appear in any others. It was this kind of bizarre task which led me to call this problem "*Calculatus Eliminatus*" as appeared in the old cartoon version of Geisel's "Cat in the Hat": one finds what one wants by finding out where it *isn't*. And that, in a nutshell, is the task.

The set-theory I used above gives a formal and unambiguous statement of these three problem classes. But I will also give you a non-technical analogy, leaving out all the biology and all the math. You have a nice fat book and you

---

[56] That is, we do not handle "improper" collections where one string is a substring of another, or which contain duplicates.

want to use it to construct a tricky puzzle, or maybe a clever sort of code. Or maybe you are writing a book and just want to have a goofy sort of index. So you ask yourself:

(1) Are there any words which appear *only* on a given page? Such a word serves as an "individual signature" for that page. Of course it may be that there aren't such words... one has to do the best one can.

(2) Are there words which appear on every page of a given chapter, and only in that chapter? These are "group signatures" for that chapter.

(3) Are there words which appear on every page, or nearly every page, of the book? These are "universal signatures" for the book.

Recently I learned a curious detail about such things. Classical scholars have long paid attention to the rarity of certain words and use the Greek phrase 'απαξ λεγομενα (*hapax legomena*) = "once[-used] words" when a certain word appears only once in a given book or author. For example, πυρσος (*pursos*) = "a torch, beacon, or signal-light," appears just once in Homer: in the *Iliad*, in Book 18 line 211. This word, therefore, acts as an *individual signature*. Words that appear just twice are called δις λεγομενα (*dis legomena*) or "twice[-used] words." Strange to say, the word δις itself is *hapax legomena*, appearing only in the *Odyssey*, in Book 9 line 491![57]

So What Happened?

I devised an experimental "radix-sort" solution to find signature strings for the rRNA collection, and with a good idea of what looked like an interesting and fruitful problem, I browsed through the journals again looking for relevant articles. Eventually I found the "complete inverted file" of Blumer *et al.* which I extended to solve the problem. In both cases, however, the wildcards had to be handled, and that made the topic very interesting.

Yet, I had to consider something: some scholars may feel that the wildcards were merely a sign of lab errors, or of some current obstacle which would eventually be overcome, thus resulting in a data collection which was only of the usual simple (non-wildcard) kind.

Hence it is necessary for us to understand a little more about why these wildcards exist in the data of molecular biology. And then, perhaps, we will have the intellectual stamina to explore their theory with the interest it deserves, which will follow.

---

[57] See Autenrieth, *A Homeric Dictionary*, 248, 78, and front matter.

4. WHY ARE THERE AMBIGUOUS BASES?

As I mentioned earlier, I found on the average that about one out of every one hundred bases in the 1991 collection of 16S rRNA sequences was a wildcard. The question was raised whether the use of wildcards was due to experimental limitations, which would eventually be transcended. The biologists, however, pointed out that while in some cases there are indeed experimental reasons which may give rise to degeneracy in a given sequence, there are other explanations which cannot be surmounted. Here are some of them:

1. Real experimental degeneracies. It must be considered that any DNA/RNA sequencing is always a "macroscopic" result – one which is visible in the discrete sense, well-defined according to practical laboratory conditions. However, this sequence is a "visible" representation (accurate as far as possible), magnified in some sense out of a sequence existing only at a molecular level in a given chromosome fragment. Errors may arise from either the magnification process or from the representation; these may not necessarily be due to "poor lab practice." For example, the usual PCR (Polymerase Chain Reaction) process of replicating a given sequence to a quantity sufficient for further processing incurs errors of copying at the rate of roughly one error in every ten million bases copied. As even the near-microscopic quantities necessary for further processing will contain hundreds of millions of copies,[58] artifacts of errors in copying may be introduced into sequences, and, in a given experiment, it may not be possible to resolve the ambiguity.

2. Real differences in the DNA sequence in various members within a given species. That is, a given base at a certain position for *one* individual may be different from the corresponding base in an equivalent position in a different individual. In some cases, these distinctions do not alter the expressed characteristics of that organism, since there are many places in the DNA sequence where there is no requirement for that base to be any particular one or another. Such bases are called *degenerate*. As can be seen from the Genetic Code in Appendix 1, most amino acids are represented by two, four, or even six codons – the triples of RNA bases which code for that amino acid. For example, in some codons, the third base (the "wobble base") may be any one of the four nucleotides, and so it is irrelevant to the meaning of that codon. We shall hear more about this case shortly.[59]

---

[58] Starting with a single molecule, thirty repeats of the Polymerase Chain Reaction (PCR) should give rise to 2^{30} or 1,073,741,824 copies. This appears to be a huge number, but since we are at the molecular level it is exceedingly tiny. Even for a sequence of about 200 bases (far larger than any useful probe), the sample would weigh about 100 picograms. Using a typical paper weight (75 grams per square meter) and printer (600dpi), 100 picograms is about 38 times smaller than a single dot of print. Modern lab technique of ultra-micro chemistry is able to handle such tiny quantities.

[59] The briefest analogy I can provide here is from programming: a typo in a comment does not cause any error, either in compilation or in execution. Note, however, that one sort of change is not permitted: there must be *some* base at that position – it may not be deleted – but which particular base is used makes no difference.

Clearly, in species which reproduce by sex, the individual will as a rule *not* have a genome identical to that of either of its parents. (Rather, it has a combination of portions of both their genomes.) However, an individual of those species (e.g. bacteria) which reproduce asexually will in general have the same sequence as its immediate ancestor. Nevertheless, there can be cases where an individual of such species may (for example) have an adenine (A) at a given location in the sequence, whereas another individual *of the same species* may have a cytosine (C) at that location, even without impairing its activity.[60] (This may happen in coding regions when there are multiple codons for the same amino acid, or when, as we indicated earlier, the base in question merely "takes up space" in the sequence though playing no operative role in the cellular machinery.)

Given the question being investigated, then, segregation of the species into separate "populations," each with a non-wildcard sequence, may be unreasonable or even impossible. (For example, there could be another divergence of population at the very next base, which is not correlated to the difference at the first base, giving rise to four sub-populations, and so on.) Hence, the sequence *must* be represented as having the appropriate wildcard: for example, M might be said to be both A and C at once. Remember that in any given single DNA sequence, which is an actually existing chemical, or arrangement of atoms, there *must* be either one or the other base at a given location: *this* individual has *this* particular nucleotide at this position – but at the macroscopic level, the sequence being studied represents a *group or collection* of individual sequences, hence a wildcard is required to express such a sequence.

(Note, however, as we shall hear shortly, certain uncommon nucleotides are actually natural wildcards.)

3. Multiple occurrences within the individual of the same sequence. This situation arises when the sequence of interest occurs more than once within the genome of the living cell – for example, the human 45S pre-rRNA component, which appears 100 times within the human genome.[61]

Pairs of these sequences may be non-identical in the mathematical sense – that is, the two may differ by one or more bases – yet they both perform identically in the biological sense. (For example, as we suggest above, it may be that the variant bases serve as "spacers" between other functional areas; that is, as long as there are the correct *number* of bases, their precise *values* are biologically indifferent.) However, researchers study areas which include such variations, so it is necessary to handle a "both/and" representation of two bases at one location.

4. The existence, whether real or experimental, of wildcards is not in itself an impediment to further work on that sequence. It is possible to synthesize sequences which have the effect of degenerate bases, up to a certain practical limit – for example, when these are to be used in *in-situ* hybridization.[62] This is done by

---

[60] Such subtle distinctions which do not impair life, growth, and replication may be termed varieties or strains of a given species. This brings up matters of taxonomy and the nature of a "species" for which we defer further exploration.

[61] Such repetitions are extremely cunning as they enable parallel processing at the molecular level. See *Molecular Cell Biology* 357.

[62] As done by the researchers whom I assisted during my doctoral work. Also see Frisher M. E., Floriani, P. J. and Nierzwicki-Baur, S. Differential sensitivity of 16S rRNA targeted

synthesizing multiple sequences, each containing the appropriate base, and using them together. As mentioned in point 2 above, the natural action of certain tRNA sequences also have the effect of matching a wildcard, as we shall mention shortly.

Clearly, then, there is some justification for the existence of wildcards, and for understanding the mathematics of strings which include them. But nature itself provides another indication of their importance: there is at least one cellular component in real living things which behaves as a wildcard.

A Real-Life Wildcard

Earlier we mentioned an example of a degenerate base in the DNA sequence, or more accurately in the working copy of the DNA sequence called the messenger RNA, mRNA. It is the blueprint from which a protein is to be built. The construction of a protein is performed by a complex cellular mechanism called the ribosome, working with transfer RNAs (tRNAs) which carry the amino acid building blocks. The mRNA is a series of triples called codons which stand for amino acids In it, the codons for certain amino acids may be two, four, or even six different DNA/RNA triples. (The complete Genetic Code is given in Appendix 1.) The degeneracy appears in the third position, which is called the "wobble base." For example, alanine is coded by any of the four codons GCA or GCC or GCG or GCT, so by using the wildcard N (which stands for *any* base) we could represent the codon for alanine with a "wildcard" string GCN.

These codons are "recognized" by a molecule called tRNA (the *t* stands for *transfer*), a part of the protein-building machinery. The tRNA has an *anti-codon* which (when read backwards) must "match" [63] the codon in the DNA sequence: the "match" being according to the Watson-Crick pairs used in the double helix:

A pairs with T in DNA, U in RNA
C pairs with G
G pairs with C
T (in DNA) pairs with A
U (in RNA) pairs with A

So in order to "match" the GCA codon for alanine, a tRNA must have the anti-codon which reads UGC.

One would expect that there have to be 64 different tRNAs, one for each of the 4·4·4 = 64 different codons (triples of the four DNA bases). However, as it turns out – and to the surprise of computer scientists – real cells use wildcards to help simplify this requirement.

For example, a tRNA may use the modified nucleotide containing *inosine* rather than one of the four usual bases. Chemically, inosine is very similar to guanine, except for the omission of an amino (NH_2) group. This base is used in the third or wobble position, and is able to match either U or C or A. This is used in the tRNA for alanine and it has the anticodon IGC.[64] That means an inosine nucleotide is nothing more than the chemical form of the "H" wildcard which represents "A" or "C" or "U". (The mnemonic for "H" is "not G.")

---

oligonucleotide, in *Canadian Journal of Microbiology* 42:1010, 1061-1071, NRC Research Press, 1996.

[63] Here the term is used in its biological sense, not the mathematical sense used elsewhere in this text.

[64] See *Molecular Cell Biology*, 92 and *Biochemistry*, 833.

Another accommodation at the wobble base of the anticodon permits two non-standard pairings:

C in the tRNA will match either A or G in the mRNA.

G in the tRNA will match either U or C in the mRNA.

Hence, certain tRNA molecules act as if their anticodon really contained the "R" (meaning "A" or "G" since these are the two purines) or the "Y" (meaning "C" or "U" which are the pyrimidines) wildcards. Granted this is partially a matter of the arrangement of the machinery, and not an actual modification as in the case of inosine; this is the wobble base, after all. But in terms of the character patterns, the effect is like those wildcards. The advantage to such things will be apparent by examining the Genetic Code in Appendix 1: several amino acids have codons in which the third base can be represented as either the "R" or "Y" wildcard.

PART II: THE THEORY OF WILDCARD ALPHABETS

We now provide the formal definitions of an extended theory of strings using alphabets containing wildcards; from a given alphabet A with $card(A) = n$ distinct characters we derive the set of *wildcards* for every possible combination of those characters. With these new symbols comes the useful and important *matches* relation and several others needed by the theory. Regardless of any practical limitations, the following definitions apply to all wildcard alphabets.

1. ELEMENTARY DEFINITIONS

Wildcard Alphabet: A *wildcard alphabet* **A** is derived from a given base alphabet A of $n = card(A)$ distinct characters. It is defined to be the set

$$\mathbf{A} = \{\mathbf{0}, \mathbf{s}_1, \mathbf{s}_2, \ldots \mathbf{s}_{z-1}\}$$

of $z = 2^n$ distinct vectors, each of n components, where each component of the vector is either zero or one. That is, for any **x** in **A**, we have

$$\mathbf{x} = \langle x_1, x_2, \ldots x_n \rangle$$

where each component x_j is either zero or one. These vectors are therefore nothing more than the binary representation of the number which is i.

By definition, for any given alphabet A, its corresponding wildcard alphabet **A** contains $2^{card(A)}$ elements.

Note that the number of possible wildcards grows exponentially as the size of the underlying base alphabet grows, and quickly becomes unwieldy: while there are only $2^4 - 1 = 15$ characters in the wildcard alphabet based on the four DNA bases, there are $2^{26} - 1 = 67,108,863$ characters in the wildcard alphabet based on a standard 26-character alphabet.

The wildcard alphabets are isomorphic to the sets of the free semigroup of subsets of a given set (that is, the base alphabet): there is exactly one such alphabet $\mathbf{A}_n$ corresponding to any base alphabet A of $n = card(A)$ characters, just as there is just one set of the free semigroup for any set with cardinality n. Some examples:

Base alphabet **Wildcard alphabet**
$A_1 = \{p\}$ $\mathbf{A}_1 = \{\langle 0 \rangle, \langle 1 \rangle\}$
$A_2 = \{p, q\}$ $\mathbf{A}_2 = \{\langle 0,0 \rangle, \langle 1,0 \rangle, \langle 0,1 \rangle, \langle 1,1 \rangle\}$
$A_3 = \{p, q, r\}$ $\mathbf{A}_3 = \{\langle 0,0,0 \rangle, \langle 1,0,0 \rangle, \langle 0,1,0 \rangle, \langle 1,1,0 \rangle,$
     $\langle 0,0,1 \rangle, \langle 1,0,1 \rangle, \langle 0,1,1 \rangle, \langle 1,1,1 \rangle\}$
$A_4 = \{p, q, r, s\}$ $\mathbf{A}_4 = \{\langle 0,0,0,0 \rangle, \langle 1,0,0,0 \rangle, \langle 0,1,0,0 \rangle, \langle 1,1,0,0 \rangle,$
     $\langle 0,0,1,0 \rangle, \langle 1,0,1,0 \rangle, \langle 0,1,1,0 \rangle, \langle 1,1,1,0 \rangle\}$
     $\langle 0,0,0,1 \rangle, \langle 1,0,0,1 \rangle, \langle 0,1,0,1 \rangle, \langle 1,1,0,1 \rangle,$
     $\langle 0,0,1,1 \rangle, \langle 1,0,1,1 \rangle, \langle 0,1,1,1 \rangle, \langle 1,1,1,1 \rangle\}$

and so forth.

For the particular needs deriving from molecular biology, we simply map the characters of A_4 to the symbols of the four DNA (or RNA) bases and write

$$A_{DNA} = \{a, c, g, t\}$$

and

$$A_{RNA} = \{a, c, g, u\}$$

Base-inclusion: A given wildcard character **x** in **A** is said to *base-include* the character a_i from the base alphabet provided that the *i*-th component of **x** is one.

Null-match: Every wildcard alphabet contains the special character
$$\mathbf{0} = <0, 0, 0, \ldots 0>$$
which is called the *null-match*. It base-includes *no* bases.

The Reduced Wildcard Alphabet: In many cases, it is convenient to exclude the null-match from consideration. Hence, we define the reduced wildcard alphabet $\mathbf{A}^-$ to be the wildcard alphabet with the null-match removed:

$$\mathbf{A}^- = \mathbf{A} - \{\mathbf{0}\}$$

Omni-match: Every wildcard alphabet contains a character **N** for which all elements are unity:
$$\mathbf{N} = <1, 1, 1, \ldots 1>$$
This character is called the *omni-match*. (The symbol **N** is mnemonic for *aNy* from the IUB codes; see Appendix 1.) It base-includes *all* bases.

Degree: The *degree* of a wildcard character **s** is the total number of characters from the base alphabet which it base-includes. This is the number of non-zero components in its vector. We may also define it to be:
$$deg(\mathbf{s}) = \Sigma\, s_i$$

Note that the degree of the null-match is zero:
$$deg(\mathbf{0}) = 0$$
and it is the only such character in the alphabet.

Also note that the degree of the omni-match character is equal to the size of the base alphabet:
$$deg(\mathbf{N}) = card(\mathbf{A})$$
It is the only such character in the wildcard alphabet, and its degree is the maximum possible for that alphabet.

For example, the wildcards of $\mathbf{A}_3$ have the following degrees:
  $deg(<0,0,0>) = 0$ (the null-match)
  $deg(<1,0,0>) = 1$
  $deg(<0,1,0>) = 1$
  $deg(<1,1,0>) = 2$
  $deg(<0,0,1>) = 1$
  $deg(<1,0,1>) = 2$
  $deg(<0,1,1>) = 2$
  $deg(<1,1,1>) = 3$ (the omni-match)

When a wildcard from a base alphabet of *n* characters is represented by a memory unit of *n* bits (typically with *n* less than or equal to the bit-size of the computer) the degree may readily be computed by the bit-count of the desired variable.

Extension: Each character a_i in A has an associated character $\eta(a_i)$ in **A** defined to be the *extension* of that character. It has the form
$$\eta(a_i) = <0, 0, \ldots 1, \ldots 0, 0>$$
where the *i*-th element is one, and all others are zero.

The extension $\eta(x)$ of any character x in A always has degree one:

$$deg(\eta(x)) = 1 \text{ for any x in A}$$

Furthermore, for any x in A, $\eta(x)$ always base-includes x, and $\eta(x)$ base-includes no other character in A.

Eigencharacter: The *card*(A) wildcards in **A** which are the extensions of the members of A are termed *eigencharacters*. (The German *eigen* means "own, particular.") That is, an eigencharacter is any symbol $\mathbf{e}_i$ in **A** which *base-includes* one and only one character e_j in A, the character of which it is the *extension*:

$\mathbf{e}_i = \eta(e_j)$.

The wildcard character $\mathbf{e}_i$ has exactly one non-zero component e_j for some *i* between 1 and *card*(A), hence it has degree 1. In any given wildcard alphabet, there are always exactly *card*(A) eigencharacters, corresponding to (as they are the extensions of) the *card*(A) characters in the base alphabet.

The Other Wildcard Characters

The remaining $2^{card(A)} - card(A) - 1$ characters of **A** (excluding the null-match and the *card*(A) eigencharacters) are the various possible "true" wildcards for A: these symbols represent *two or more* distinct characters in A. For example, $\mathbf{a}_3 = <1,1,0,\ldots 0>$ represents either a_1 or a_2.

Such wildcards permit us to arrange various sorts of restrictions or generalizations about strings, not simply in the sense that we wish to find a substring in the base alphabet which matches some wildcard-containing query, but also to explore the characteristics of degenerate data which itself contains wildcards, as occurs in actual DNA and RNA sequences of molecular biology.

Equality: Two characters in the wildcard alphabet **A** are *equal* if and only if each of the *card*(A) components of the two characters are equal.

For any **x** and **y** in **A**, we write **x** = **y** provided that
$$x_i = y_i \text{ for } 1 \leq i \leq card(A)$$

Note that this is *not* the "matches" relation which we shall define presently; this is a *strict* equality, which is
    reflexive, since **x** = **x** for any **x** in **A**
    symmetric, since **x** = **y** implies **y** = **x** for any **x** and **y** in **A**
    and transitive, since **x** = **y** and **y** = **z** implies **x** = **z** for any **x**, **y**, **z** in **A**
These properties follow from the properties of the equality of the components.

Inclusion: (Note that this is *not* the same relation as base-inclusion.)

For two wildcard characters **x** and **y** in **A**, we say **x** *includes* **y**, written:

$$\mathbf{x} \supseteq \mathbf{y}$$

if and only if whenever y_i is one, x_i is also one. That is, $\mathbf{x} \supseteq \mathbf{y}$ provided that

$$y_i = 1 \text{ implies } x_i = 1 \text{ for } 1 \leq i \leq card(A).$$

To say that **x** *includes* **y** means that **x** must base-include every character which **y** base-includes, though it may base-include others as well.

The *includes* relation can be computed by the following Boolean equation:

$$\mathbf{x} \supseteq \mathbf{y} = \bigcap_{i=1}^{|A|} \neg y_i \vee x_i$$

The important *includes* relation is reflexive, antisymmetric, and transitive:

Proof of reflexivity: We must show that for any **x** in **A**, $\mathbf{x} \supseteq \mathbf{x}$.
   Trivial, since for every **x** in **A**, $x_i = 1$ implies $x_i = 1$ for $1 \leq i \leq card(A)$.
   Thus, $\mathbf{x} \supseteq \mathbf{x}$.

Proof of antisymmetry: We must show that for any **x**, **y** in **A** with $\mathbf{x} \neq \mathbf{y}$, $\mathbf{x} \supseteq \mathbf{y}$ implies that $\mathbf{y} \supseteq \mathbf{x}$ is false.
   Given any **x**, **y** in **A** with $\mathbf{x} \neq \mathbf{y}$ and $\mathbf{x} \supseteq \mathbf{y}$. Since $\mathbf{x} \neq \mathbf{y}$ there must be some k with $1 \leq k \leq card(A)$ for which $x_k \neq y_k$. Also, since $\mathbf{x} \supseteq \mathbf{y}$, we know that there is no component for which $x_j = 0$ and $y_j = 1$ for any j with $1 \leq j \leq card(A)$. Hence, in the case where $x_k \neq y_k$ it can only be the case that $x_j = 1$ and $y_j = 0$.
   Then, evaluating the truth of $\mathbf{y} \supseteq \mathbf{x}$ using the above iterated AND (note that the variables are interchanged!) at $i = k$ we have

$$\neg x_j \vee y_j$$

or

$$\neg 1 \vee 0$$

which is 0. Any AND with a false term is itself false, hence the iterated AND is false, so we have shown $\mathbf{y} \supseteq \mathbf{x}$ is false.

Proof of transitivity: We must show that for any **x**, **y**, **z** in **A**, $\mathbf{x} \supseteq \mathbf{y}$ and $\mathbf{y} \supseteq \mathbf{z}$ implies that $\mathbf{x} \supseteq \mathbf{z}$.
   Given any **x**, **y**, **z** in **A** with $\mathbf{x} \supseteq \mathbf{y}$ and $\mathbf{y} \supseteq \mathbf{z}$. Assume the contrary, that $\mathbf{x} \supseteq \mathbf{z}$ is false. That means there must be some component where $x_k = 0$ and $z_k = 1$ for $1 \leq k \leq card(A)$. Since $z_k = 1$ and $\mathbf{y} \supseteq \mathbf{z}$, we must have $y_k = 1$. But then, since $\mathbf{x} \supseteq \mathbf{y}$, we must also have $x_k = 1$. Which is contrary to our assumption.
   Hence we must have $\mathbf{x} \supseteq \mathbf{z}$.

The *includes* relation forms a *partial order* on the wildcard alphabet

Since the *includes* relation is reflexive, antisymmetric, and transitive, it forms a *partial order* on the underlying set.

We here observe a curious detail about this partial order: except for the trivial case where the base alphabet has exactly one character (hence its wildcard alphabet has only two characters, the null-match **0** and the omni-match **N**), *all* wildcard alphabets contain characters which *neither* include another character, *nor* are included by another.

For example, consider the base alphabet $A_{pq} = \{p, q\}$. The corresponding wildcard alphabet is $\mathbf{A}_{pq} = \{\mathbf{0}, \mathbf{p}, \mathbf{q}, \mathbf{N}\}$

$\mathbf{0} = <0,0>$ the null-match
$\mathbf{p} = <1,0>$ eigencharacter for p
$\mathbf{q} = <0,1>$ eigencharacter for q
$\mathbf{N} = <1,1>$ the omni-match

Clearly,

$\mathbf{N} \supseteq \mathbf{p}$ since both **N** and **p** base-includes p, and
$\mathbf{N} \supseteq \mathbf{q}$ since both **N** and **q** base-includes q,

however, both $\mathbf{p} \supseteq \mathbf{q}$ and $\mathbf{q} \supseteq \mathbf{p}$ are false.

In other words, neither of the statements "**p** includes **q**" nor "**q** includes **p**" is true.

Broad: The relation *broad*(**x**, **y**) for a pair of given wildcards yields the wildcard of *minimal* degree which includes both **x** and **y**. It is defined to be the component-wise logical OR of the components of the two wildcards:

$$broad(\mathbf{x}, \mathbf{y}) = <x_1 \vee y_1, x_2 \vee y_2, ... x_{card(A)} \vee y_{card(A)}>$$

We note that for any wildcards **x**, **y**, **z**,
$broad(\mathbf{x}, broad(\mathbf{y}, \mathbf{z})) = broad(broad(\mathbf{x}, \mathbf{y}), \mathbf{z})$
$broad(\mathbf{x}, \mathbf{y}) = broad(\mathbf{y}, \mathbf{x})$
$broad(\mathbf{x}, \mathbf{x}) = \mathbf{x}$
$broad(\mathbf{x}, \mathbf{0}) = \mathbf{x}$

That is, *broad* is associative, commutative, idempotent, and has an identity **0**.

Narrow: The relation *narrow*(**x**, **y**) for a pair of given wildcards yields the wildcard of *maximal* degree which is included by both **x** and **y**. It is defined to be the component-wise logical AND of the components of the two wildcards:

$$narrow(\mathbf{x}, \mathbf{y}) = <x_1 \wedge y_1, x_2 \wedge y_2, ... x_{card(A)} \wedge y_{card(A)}>$$

We note that for any wildcards **x**, **y**, **z**,
$narrow(\mathbf{x}, narrow(\mathbf{y}, \mathbf{z})) = narrow(narrow(\mathbf{x}, \mathbf{y}), \mathbf{z})$
$narrow(\mathbf{x}, \mathbf{y}) = narrow(\mathbf{y}, \mathbf{x})$
$narrow(\mathbf{x}, \mathbf{x}) = \mathbf{x}$
$narrow(\mathbf{x}, \mathbf{N}) = \mathbf{x}$

That is, *narrow* is associative, commutative, idempotent, and has an identity **N**.

Lattice: The algebraic structure $\langle \mathbf{A}, \supseteq, narrow, broad \rangle$ is a lattice, since is a partial order and has both a least upper bound and greatest lower bound:

broad is the least upper bound for **A**, since for $\mathbf{z} = broad(\mathbf{x},\mathbf{y})$, we have
$(\mathbf{w} \supseteq \mathbf{x})$ and $(\mathbf{w} \supseteq \mathbf{y})$ implies $(\mathbf{w} \supseteq \mathbf{z})$ for all **w** in **A**.

narrow is the greatest lower bound for **A**, since for $\mathbf{z} = narrow(\mathbf{x},\mathbf{y})$, we have
$(\mathbf{x} \supseteq \mathbf{w})$ and $(\mathbf{y} \supseteq \mathbf{w})$ implies $(\mathbf{z} \supseteq \mathbf{w})$ for all **w** in **A**.

Distributivity: We note that *narrow* distributes over *broad*, and *broad* over *narrow*.

$$narrow(\mathbf{x}, broad(\mathbf{y}, \mathbf{z})) = broad(narrow(\mathbf{x}, \mathbf{y}), narrow(\mathbf{x}, \mathbf{z}))$$

$$broad(\mathbf{x}, narrow(\mathbf{y}, \mathbf{z})) = narrow(broad(\mathbf{x}, \mathbf{y}), broad(\mathbf{x}, \mathbf{z}))$$

Furthermore, the *absorption rules* hold:
$$narrow(\mathbf{x}, broad(\mathbf{x}, \mathbf{y})) = \mathbf{x}$$
and
$$broad(\mathbf{x}, narrow(\mathbf{x}, \mathbf{y})) = \mathbf{x}$$

Negative: The *negative* of a given wildcard character **x** in **A** yields the wildcard for which the components are the Boolean complement of the components of **x**:

$$-\mathbf{x} = \langle \neg x_1, \neg x_2, \ldots \neg x_{card(A)} \rangle$$

We note that for any wildcard **x**:
If $\mathbf{y} = -\mathbf{x}$, then $\mathbf{x} = -\mathbf{y}$.
Also, $-(-\mathbf{x}) = \mathbf{x}$.

Boolean Algebra: Since the algebraic structure $\langle \mathbf{A}, \supseteq, narrow, broad, -\rangle$ is a distributive lattice with a complement, it is a Boolean Algebra.

The *matches* relation: If two wildcard characters both base-include the same character, they are said to *match*. The *matches* relation $\mathbf{x} \approx \mathbf{y}$ for any **x** and **y** in the wildcard alphabet **A** is defined to be:

$\mathbf{x} \approx \mathbf{y}$ if and only if both $x_i = 1$ and $y_i = 1$ for some i with $1 \leq i \leq card(A)$.

Note that there may be *more than one* such value of i, in the case where both wildcard characters base-include more than one character of the base alphabet.
 Also note that the null-match **0** matches *no* other character, as expected. It may seem curious, but by the definition it does not match itself, either.

The *matches* relation can be computed by the following Boolean equation:

$$\mathbf{x} \approx \mathbf{y} = \bigcup_{i=1}^{card(A)} x_i \wedge y_i$$

A practical note: if *card*(A) is not larger than the word size of the machine on which one desires to implement this relation, one may assign the characters of the base alphabet A to the bits of the machine word. Hence, the *matches* relation is simply a test for zero/non-zero of the bit-wise AND of the two arguments, thus dropping its computational complexity from *card*(A) to constant.

Properties of the matches relation:

1. The *matches* relation is reflexive over the reduced wildcard alphabet: **x≈x** for any **x** in **A⁻**. This follows from the definition.

2. The *matches* relation is symmetric. If **x≈y** then **y≈x**. This follows from transposing x and y in the definition.

3. The *matches* relation is **not** transitive. This is readily shown by counterexample. Consider the base alphabet A = {p, q}. Then the corresponding wildcard alphabet **A** = {**0**, **p**, **q**, **N**} where **0** is the null-match, **N** is the omni-match, and **p** and **q** are the eigencharacters which are the extensions of the two base characters. Obviously p≈N and N≈q, but it is *not* true that p≈q.

In our example alphabet, we merely note that **A≈M** and **M≈C**, but it is *not true* that **A≈C**. There are a number of other such examples in **A**$_{DNA}$.

It is very important to note this lack of transitivity, as it has significant ramifications in algorithms which use the *matches* relation, as we shall explore in detail in the case of applying the KMP algorithm to strings containing wildcards, later in this book.

2. Strings over a Wildcard Alphabet

Just as strings are formed from a given (base) alphabet A by concatenation producing the star-closure A* of that alphabet, we form strings from a wildcard alphabet **A** by concatenation, producing its star-closure **A***. Several additional relations and functions will be useful.

Wildcard String: Given a wildcard alphabet **A**, a string σ is a finite sequence of characters of **A**:

$$\sigma = \sigma_1 \sigma_2 \sigma_3 \ldots \sigma_{len(\sigma)}$$

where each σ_i is a character in **A**.

String length: The length of σ is given by $len(\sigma)$, as for strings over the base alphabet.

Concatenation

The operator • over the wildcard alphabet **A** performs the *concatenation* of two strings over **A**, as for strings over the base alphabet.

Given two (possibly empty) strings $\sigma = \sigma_1\sigma_2\ldots\sigma_{len(\sigma)}$ and $\tau = \tau_1\tau_2\ldots\tau_{len(\tau)}$, we define the concatenation $\sigma \bullet \tau$ to be the string of length $len(\sigma) + len(\tau)$ in which all the characters from σ appear in order, followed by all of the characters from τ in order:

$$\sigma \bullet \tau = \sigma_1\sigma_2\ldots\sigma_{len(\sigma)} \tau_1\tau_2\ldots\tau_{len(\tau)}$$

Eigenstring

A wildcard string σ is defined to be an *eigenstring* if every one of its characters is an eigencharacter in the wildcard alphabet. That is,

$$deg(\sigma_i) = 1 \text{ for } 1 \leq i \leq len(\sigma)$$

The *includes* relation

A wildcard string σ is said to *include* another wildcard string τ, written

$$\sigma \supseteq \tau$$

provided that
$$len(\sigma) = len(\tau)$$
and
$$\sigma_i \supseteq \tau_i \text{ for } 1 \leq i \leq len(\sigma)$$

Since the *includes* relation for wildcards is transitive, the *includes* relation for strings is likewise transitive: $\sigma \supseteq \tau$ and $\tau \supseteq \upsilon$ implies $\sigma \supseteq \upsilon$ for any strings σ, τ, υ.

Multiplicity

The multiplicity $M(\sigma)$ of a wildcard string σ is defined to be the number of distinct eigenstrings it includes. Since a wildcard **s** base-includes $deg(\mathbf{s})$ distinct characters of the base alphabet, the multiplicity of a string can be computed by:

$$M(\sigma) = \prod_{i=1}^{|\sigma|} \deg(\sigma_i)$$

The multiplicity of every eigenstring is one.

Inclusion-set

Given a wildcard string σ, its inclusion set I(σ) is defined to be the set of all strings over the wildcard alphabet which σ includes:

$$I(\sigma) = \{ \beta \mid \sigma \supseteq \beta \}$$

Eigen-inclusion-set

Given a wildcard string σ, its eigen-inclusion-set E(σ) is defined to be the set of all eigenstrings over the wildcard alphabet which σ includes:

$$E(\sigma) = \{ \beta \mid \sigma \supseteq \beta \text{ and } M(\beta)=1 \}$$

Note that for any string σ,

$$card(E(\sigma)) = M(\sigma)$$

Also note that if σ is an eigenstring, M(σ) = 1 hence:

$$E(\sigma) = \{ \sigma \}$$

The *matches* relation

This relation is simply the extension of the *matches* relation over the wildcard alphabet to strings over that alphabet.

Two wildcard strings are said to *match*, written

$$\sigma \approx \tau$$

provided that

$$len(\sigma) = len(\tau)$$

and

$$\sigma_i \approx \tau_i \text{ for } 1 \leq i \leq len(\sigma)$$

Alternatively, σ ≈ τ if and only if there exists an eigenstring θ which both strings include:

σ ≈ τ if and only if $\sigma \supseteq \theta$ and $\tau \supseteq \theta$ and $M(\theta) = 1$ for some θ in **A***

Here we call attention to the fact that the *matches* relation is *not* transitive: if σ ≈ τ and τ ≈ υ, it is not necessarily the case that σ ≈ υ. This follows from the non-transitivity of the *matches* relation for characters in the wildcard alphabet.

3. WILDCARDS FOR A TWO-CHARACTER BASE ALPHABET

The simplest wildcard alphabet derives from an alphabet of *two* characters, and so it is a Boolean Algebra of size four. Let A = {a, b}.
Then we have the corresponding (reduced) wildcard alphabet **A**:

A = {**a**, **b**, **n**}

They are the two extensions of the base characters

$\mathbf{a} = \eta(a) = <1,0>$
$\mathbf{b} = \eta(b) = <0,1>$

and the omni-match

$\mathbf{n} = <1,1>$.

Due to its simplicity, the two characters a and b are "negatives" of each other, since

$-\mathbf{a} = \neg<1,0> = <0,1> = \mathbf{b}$

and

$-\mathbf{b} = \neg<0,1> = <1,0> = \mathbf{a}$

Here is the Hasse diagram for this Boolean Algebra:

The wild characters match according to the following table:

	a	**b**	**n**
a	1	0	1
b	0	1	1
n	1	1	1

There are nine strings of length 2 over this alphabet, which match the following:

```
string  count   matching
  aa      4     aa an na nn
  ab      4     ab an nb nn
  an      6     aa ab an na nb nn
  ba      4     ba bn na nn
  bb      4     bb bn nb nn
  bn      6     ba bb bn na nb nn
  na      6     aa an ba bn na nn
  nb      6     ab an bb bn nb nn
  nn      9     aa ab an ba bb bn na nb nn
```

Observe that there are three classes of matches:
strings with multiplicity 1 have 4 matches: aa ab ba bb
strings with multiplicity 2 have 6 matches: an bn na nb
strings with multiplicity 4 have 9 matches: nn

4. WILDCARDS FOR A THREE-CHARACTER BASE ALPHABET

The wildcard alphabet deriving from an alphabet of *three* characters is a Boolean Algebra of size eight. Let $A_3 = \{a, b, c\}$.
Then we have the corresponding (reduced) wildcard alphabet **A₃**:
  A₃ = {**a, b, c, x, y, z, n**}
There are the three extensions of the base characters,
  $\mathbf{a} = \eta(a) = <1,0,0>$
  $\mathbf{b} = \eta(b) = <0,1,0>$
  $\mathbf{c} = \eta(c) = <0,0,1>$
the three negatives of these characters:
  $\mathbf{x} = <0,1,1> = -\mathbf{a}$
  $\mathbf{y} = <1,0,1> = -\mathbf{b}$
  $\mathbf{z} = <1,1,0> = -\mathbf{c}$
and the omni-match,
  $\mathbf{n} = <1,1,1>$.

Here is its Hasse diagram:

The wild characters match according to the following table:

	a	b	c	x	y	z	n
a	1	0	1	0	1	0	1
b	0	1	1	0	0	1	1
c	1	1	1	0	1	1	1
x	0	0	0	1	1	1	1
y	1	0	1	1	1	1	1
z	0	1	1	1	1	1	1
n	1	1	1	1	1	1	1

There are 49 strings of length 2 over this alphabet, which match the following:

```
string count  matching
aa    16    aa az ay an za zz zy zn ya yz yy yn na nz ny nn
ab    16    ab az ax an zb zz zx zn yb yz yx yn nb nz nx nn
az    24    aa ab az ay ax an za zb zz zy zx zn ya yb yz yy
            yx yn na nb nz ny nx nn
ac    16    ac ay ax an zc zy zx zn yc yy yx yn nc ny nx nn
ay    24    aa az ac ay ax an za zz zc zy zx zn ya yz yc yy
            yx yn na nz nc ny nx nn
ax    24    ab az ac ay ax an zb zz zc zy zx zn yb yz yc yy
            yx yn nb nz nc ny nx nn
an    28    aa ab az ac ay ax an za zb zz zc zy zx zn ya yb
            yz yc yy yx yn na nb nz nc ny nx nn
```

```
ba  16   ba bz by bn za zz zy zn xa xz xy xn na nz ny nn
bb  16   bb bz bx bn zb zz zx zn xb xz xx xn nb nz nx nn
bz  24   ba bb bz by bx bn za zb zz zy zx zn xa xb xz xy
         xx xn na nb nz ny nx nn
bc  16   bc by bx bn zc zy zx zn xc xy xx xn nc ny nx nn
by  24   ba bz bc by bx bn za zz zc zy zx zn xa xz xc xy
         xx xn na nz nc ny nx nn
bx  24   bb bz bc by bx bn zb zz zc zy zx zn xb xz xc xy
         xx xn nb nz nc ny nx nn
bn  28   ba bb bz bc by bx bn za zb zz zc zy zx zn xa xb
         xz xc xy xx xn na nb nz nc ny nx nn
za  24   aa az ay an ba bz by bn za zz zy zn ya yz yy yn
         xa xz xy xn na nz ny nn
zb  24   ab az ax an bb bz bx bn zb zz zx zn yb yz yx yn
         xb xz xx xn nb nz nx nn
zz  36   aa ab az ay ax an ba bb bz by bx bn za zb zz zy
         zx zn ya yb yz yy yx yn xa xb xz xy xx xn na nb
         nz ny nx nn
zc  24   ac ay ax an bc by bx bn zc zy zx zn yc yy yx yn
         xc xy xx xn nc ny nx nn
zy  36   aa az ac ay ax an ba bz bc by bx bn za zz zc zy
         zx zn ya yz yc yy yx yn xa xz xc xy xx xn na nz
         nc ny nx nn
zx  36   ab az ac ay ax an bb bz bc by bx bn zb zz zc zy
         zx zn yb yz yc yy yx yn xb xz xc xy xx xn nb nz
         nc ny nx nn
zn  42   aa ab az ac ay ax an ba bb bz bc by bx bn za zb
         zz zc zy zx zn ya yb yz yc yy yx yn xa xb xz xc
         xy xx xn na nb nz nc ny nx nn
ca  16   ca cz cy cn ya yz yy yn xa xz xy xn na nz ny nn
cb  16   cb cz cx cn yb yz yx yn xb xz xx xn nb nz nx nn
cz  24   ca cb cz cy cx cn ya yb yz yy yx yn xa xb xz xy
         xx xn na nb nz ny nx nn
cc  16   cc cy cx cn yc yy yx yn xc xy xx xn nc ny nx nn
cy  24   ca cz cc cy cx cn ya yz yc yy yx yn xa xz xc xy
         xx xn na nz nc ny nx nn
cx  24   cb cz cc cy cx cn yb yz yc yy yx yn xb xz xc xy
         xx xn nb nz nc ny nx nn
cn  28   ca cb cz cc cy cx cn ya yb yz yc yy yx yn xa xb
         xz xc xy xx xn na nb nz nc ny nx nn
ya  24   aa az ay an za zz zy zn ca cz cy cn ya yz yy yn
         xa xz xy xn na nz ny nn
yb  24   ab az ax an zb zz zx zn cb cz cx cn yb yz yx yn
         xb xz xx xn nb nz nx nn
yz  36   aa ab az ay ax an za zb zz zy zx zn ca cb cz cy
         cx cn ya yb yz yy yx yn xa xb xz xy xx xn na nb
         nz ny nx nn
yc  24   ac ay ax an zc zy zx zn cc cy cx cn yc yy yx yn
         xc xy xx xn nc ny nx nn
yy  36   aa az ac ay ax an za zz zc zy zx zn ca cz cc cy
         cx cn ya yz yc yy yx yn xa xz xc xy xx xn na nz
         nc ny nx nn
yx  36   ab az ac ay ax an zb zz zc zy zx zn cb cz cc cy
         cx cn yb yz yc yy yx yn xb xz xc xy xx xn nb nz
         nc ny nx nn
```

```
yn  42   aa ab az ac ay ax an za zb zz zc zy zx zn ca cb
         cz cc cy cx cn ya yb yz yc yy yx yn xa xb xz xc
         xy xx xn na nb nz nc ny nx nn
xa  24   ba bz by bn za zz zy zn ca cz cy cn ya yz yy yn
         xa xz xy xn na nz ny nn
xb  24   bb bz bx bn zb zz zx zn cb cz cx cn yb yz yx yn
         xb xz xx xn nb nz nx nn
xz  36   ba bb bz by bx bn za zb zz zy zx zn ca cb cz cy
         cx cn ya yb yz yy yx yn xa xb xz xy xx xn na nb
         nz ny nx nn
xc  24   bc by bx bn zc zy zx zn cc cy cx cn yc yy yx yn
         xc xy xx xn nc ny nx nn
xy  36   ba bz bc by bx bn za zz zc zy zx zn ca cz cc cy
         cx cn ya yz yc yy yx yn xa xz xc xy xx xn na nz
         nc ny nx nn
xx  36   bb bz bc by bx bn zb zz zc zy zx zn cb cz cc cy
         cx cn yb yz yc yy yx yn xb xz xc xy xx xn nb nz
         nc ny nx nn
xn  42   ba bb bz bc by bx bn za zb zz zc zy zx zn ca cb
         cz cc cy cx cn ya yb yz yc yy yx yn xa xb xz xc
         xy xx xn na nb nz nc ny nx nn
na  28   aa az ay an ba bz by bn za zz zy zn ca cz cy cn
         ya yz yy yn xa xz xy xn na nz ny nn
nb  28   ab az ax an bb bz bx bn zb zz zx zn cb cz cx cn
         yb yz yx yn xb xz xx xn nb nz nx nn
nz  42   aa ab az ay ax an ba bb bz by bx bn za zb zz zy
         zx zn ca cb cz cy cx cn ya yb yz yy yx yn xa xb
         xz xy xx xn na nb nz ny nx nn
nc  28   ac ay ax an bc by bx bn zc zy zx zn cc cy cx cn
         yc yy yx yn xc xy xx xn nc ny nx nn
ny  42   aa az ac ay ax an ba bz bc by bx bn za zz zc zy
         zx zn ca cz cc cy cx cn ya yz yc yy yx yn xa xz
         xc xy xx xn na nz nc ny nx nn
nx  42   ab az ac ay ax an bb bz bc by bx bn zb zz zc zy
         zx zn cb cz cc cy cx cn yb yz yc yy yx yn xb xz
         xc xy xx xn nb nz nc ny nx nn
nn  49   aa ab az ac ay ax an ba bb bz bc by bx bn za zb
         zz zc zy zx zn ca cb cz cc cy cx cn ya yb yz yc
         yy yx yn xa xb xz xc xy xx xn na nb nz nc ny nx
         nn
```

However, unlike the previous case, there are *six* classes of matches:

```
mult    matches    strings
  1       16       aa ab ac ba bb bc ca cb cc
  2       24       az ay ax bz by bx za zb zc cz cy cx
                   ya yb yc xa xb xc
  3       28       an bn cn na nb nc
  4       36       zz zy zx yz yy yx xz xy xx
  6       42       zn yn xn nz ny nx
  9       49       nn
```

5. WILDCARDS FOR A FOUR-CHARACTER BASE ALPHABET

The wildcard alphabet deriving from an alphabet of four characters is a Boolean Algebra of size 16. Rather than show a general version, we shall use the DNA symbols as our base alphabet.

The base alphabet for DNA

Let $A_{DNA} = \{a, c, g, t\}$. These are merely the initial letters of the four biological nucleotides – adenine, cytosine, guanine, and thymine – organic ring compounds of carbon, nitrogen, oxygen, and hydrogen.

We should here point out that for most typical applications of computing to biological sequences, we will either be working exclusively with DNA sequences, *or* with RNA sequences, though there are issues in biochemistry and molecular biology in which one may encounter anomalous bases,[65] these do not arise in typical computational problems about those sequences as such.

As a matter of practicality I prefer to use the following mapping from the DNA bases to bits:

base	bits	integer	WC
a	00	0	t
c	01	1	g
g	10	2	c
t	11	3	a

This has the advantage of being alphabetical, so it is easy to remember. It also yields an easy computation of the Watson-Crick complement (WC in above table), either by a bit-wise complement, or by subtraction of the mapped integer from 3. This mapping also simplifies the arrangement of the wildcard alphabet, which we will now examine.

From this DNA base alphabet we have the corresponding (reduced) wildcard alphabet A_{DNA}:

$A_{DNA} = \{A, C, M, G, R, S, V, T, W, Y, H, K, D, B, N\}$

This alphabet has four classes of wildcards:

1. the four extensions of the base characters, the eigencharacters:
   $A = \eta(a) = <1,0,0,0>$
   $C = \eta(c) = <0,1,0,0>$
   $G = \eta(g) = <0,0,1,0>$
   $T = \eta(t) = <0,0,0,1>$

---

[65] Here are just two examples: (1) Transfer RNA, tRNA, may use thymine, as well as highly modified nucleotides such as inosine, pseudouradine, dihydrouradine and others. See Darnell, *et al.*, *Molecular Cell Biology*, 91. Recall our earlier comment that inosine may act as a biochemical "H" wildcard. (2) The erroneous hydrolytic deamination of cytosine in DNA which results in a uracil. Such DNA is damaged and can be repaired since uracil is not used in DNA. See Rawn, *Biochemistry*, 730-34.

2. the four negatives[66] of these characters:
   $-A = B = <0,1,1,1>$
   $-C = D = <1,0,1,1>$
   $-G = H = <1,1,0,1>$
   $-T = V = <1,1,1,0>$
3. six wildcards matching the six different *pairs* of base extensions:
   $M = <1,1,0,0> = -K$
   $K = <0,0,1,1> = -M$
   $S = <0,1,1,0> = -W$
   $W = <1,0,0,1> = -S$
   $R = <1,0,1,0> = -Y$
   $Y = <0,1,0,1> = -R$
4. and the omni-match
   $N = <1,1,1,1>$.

As can be seen from the above, there is a simple relation from the proposed mapping of the base alphabet to a related one for the wildcard alphabet. The mapping for the wildcard w for two bases with mappings p and q is computed by

$$w = (1 \text{ SHIFT-LEFT } p) \text{ OR } (1 \text{ SHIFT-LEFT } q)$$

(Don't be confused by the seems to be a reversal of codes; it's an "endian" thing. The notation for the wildcard $A = <1,0,0,0>$ stands for the *same entity* as the bit representation 0001.)

For reference, here is the table for the wildcard mappings:

Wildcard	bit	integer	base-includes
A	0001	1	a
C	0010	2	c
M	0011	3	a, c
G	0100	4	g
R	0101	5	a, g
S	0110	6	c, g
V	0111	7	a, c, g
T	1000	8	t
W	1001	9	a, t
Y	1010	10	c, t
H	1011	11	a, c, t
K	1100	12	g, t
D	1101	13	a, g, t
B	1110	14	c, g, t
N	1111	15	a, c, g, t

---

[66] Note that these "negatives" are those of the wildcard algebra, and *not* the Watson-Crick complements, represented as ~x and used in certain other studies of these sequences: ~a = t and ~c = g for A_{DNA}; ~a = u and ~c = g for A_{RNA}.

The following is the Hasse diagram for the DNA wildcard alphabet, A_{DNA}:

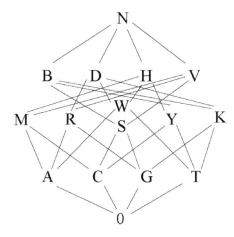

Note that the 16 wildcards of A_{DNA} are at the "corners" of a 4-dimensional hypercube.

Just for reference, here are some properties of these wildcards:

wildcard	degree	base-includes	includes
0	0	∅	∅
A	1	a	A
C	1	c	C
M	2	a, c	A, C, M
G	1	g	G
R	2	a, g	A, G, R
S	2	c, g	C, G, S
V	3	a, c, g	A, C, M, G, R, S, V
T	1	t	T
W	2	a, t	A, T
Y	2	c, t	C, T
H	3	a, c, t	A, C, M, T, W, Y, H
K	2	g, t	G, T, K
D	3	a, g, t	A, G, R, T, W, K, D
B	3	c, g, t	C, G, S, T, Y, K, B
N	4	a, c, g, t	A, C, M, G, R, S, V, T, W, Y, H, K, D, B, N

The wild characters match according to the following table:

	A	C	M	G	R	S	V	T	W	Y	H	K	D	B	N
A	1	0	1	0	1	0	1	0	1	0	1	0	1	0	1
C	0	1	1	0	0	1	1	0	0	1	1	0	0	1	1
M	1	1	1	0	1	1	1	0	1	1	1	0	1	1	1
G	0	0	0	1	1	1	1	0	0	0	0	1	1	1	1
R	1	0	1	1	1	1	1	0	1	0	1	1	1	1	1
S	0	1	1	1	1	1	1	0	0	1	1	1	1	1	1
V	1	1	1	1	1	1	1	0	1	1	1	1	1	1	1
T	0	0	0	0	0	0	0	1	1	1	1	1	1	1	1
W	1	0	1	0	1	0	1	1	1	1	1	1	1	1	1
Y	0	1	1	0	0	1	1	1	1	1	1	1	1	1	1
H	1	1	1	0	1	1	1	1	1	1	1	1	1	1	1
K	0	0	0	1	1	1	1	1	1	1	1	1	1	1	1
D	1	0	1	1	1	1	1	1	1	1	1	1	1	1	1
B	0	1	1	1	1	1	1	1	1	1	1	1	1	1	1
N	1	1	1	1	1	1	1	1	1	1	1	1	1	1	1

There are 225 strings of length 2 over this alphabet, the matching (mat) of which may be organized into the following ten classes depending on the *detailed multiplicity* (mu) of the strings.

```
mu  mat  strings
 1   64  aa ac ag at ca cc cg ct ga gc gg gt ta tc tg tt
 2   96  am ar as aw ay ak cm cr cs cw cy ck ma mc mg mt
         gm gr gs gw gy gk ra rc rg rt sa sc sg st tm tr
         ts tw ty tk wa wc wg wt ya yc yg yt ka kc kg kt
 3  112  av ah ad ab cv ch cd cb gv gh gd gb va vc vg vt
         tv th td tb ha hc hg ht da dc dg dt ba bc bg bt
 4  120  an cn gn tn na nc ng nt
 4  144  mm mr ms mw my mk rm rr rs rw ry rk sm sr ss sw
         sy sk wm wr ws ww wy wk ym yr ys yw yy yk km kr
         ks kw ky kk
 6  168  mv mh md mb rv rh rd rb sv sh sd sb vm vr vs vw
         vy vk wv wh wd wb yv yh yd yb hm hr hs hw hy hk
         kv kh kd kb dm dr ds dw dy dk bm br bs bw by bk
 8  180  mn rn sn wn yn kn nm nr ns nw ny nk
 9  196  vv vh vd vb hv hh hd hb dv dh dd db bv bh bd bb
12  210  vn hn dn bn nv nh nd nb
16  225  nn
```

We now begin to see some of the intricacy of this particular alphabet: note that while both **an** and **mm** have multiplicity 4, **mm** matches 144 strings:

```
aa ac am ar as av aw ay ah ad ab an ca cc cm cr cs cv cw cy ch cd cb
cn ma mc mm mr ms mv mw my mh md mb mn ra rc rm rr rs rv rw ry rh rd
rb rn sa sc sm sr ss sv sw sy sh sd sb sn va vc vm vr vs vv vw vy vh
vd vb vn wa wc wm wr ws wv ww wy wh wd wb wn ya yc ym yr ys yv yw yy
yh yd yb yn ha hc hm hr hs hv hw hy hh hd hb hn da dc dm dr ds dv dw
dy dh dd db dn ba bc bm br bs bv bw by bh bd bb bn na nc nm nr ns nv
nw ny nh nd nb nn
```

However, **an** only matches 120:

```
aa ac am ag ar as av at aw ay ah ak ad ab an ma mc mm mg mr ms mv mt
mw my mh mk md mb mn ra rc rm rg rr rs rv rt rw ry rh rk rd rb rn va
vc vm vg vr vs vv vt vw vy vh vk vd vb vn wa wc wm wg wr ws wv wt ww
wy wh wk wd wb wn ha hc hm hg hr hs hv ht hw hy hh hk hd hb hn da dc
dm dg dr ds dv dt dw dy dh dk dd db dn na nc nm ng nr ns nv nt nw ny
nh nk nd nb nn
```

6. WILDCARDS FOR A FIVE-CHARACTER BASE ALPHABET

The wildcard alphabet deriving from an alphabet of five characters is a Boolean Algebra of size 32. Its Hasse diagram is a hypercube in five dimensions,[67] which is not very easy to grasp when it is reduced to two, so we have omitted the labels:

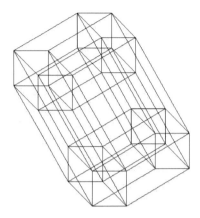

We use the first five capital letters along with all 26 lower-case letters to represent the 31 non-null wildcards as in the following table:

```
0   0  00000    D   1  00010    E   1  00001    v   2  00011
A   1  10000    j   2  10010    p   2  10001    w   3  10011
B   1  01000    k   2  01010    q   2  01001    x   3  01011
f   2  11000    l   3  11010    r   3  11001    c   4  11011
C   1  00100    m   2  00110    s   2  00101    y   3  00111
g   2  10100    n   3  10110    t   3  10101    b   4  10111
h   2  01100    o   3  01110    u   3  01101    a   4  01111
i   3  11100    e   4  11110    d   4  11101    N   5  11111
```

Note also along with the five extensions of the base characters (ABCDE), their five negatives (abcde) with degree 4, and the omni-match (N) of degree 5, there are ten wildcards of degree 2 (fghjkmpqsv); their ten inverses (ilnortuwxy) with degree 3. Among the interesting features of this set is the distribution of the matchings of a two-character string, but as there are 961 of these, we only present the summary on the following page.

---

[67] It has been noted that few Earthings care to (are able to?) handle geometry in dimensions above three, which perhaps accounts for their lack of interstellar flight. Ah well; they'll learn eventually.

```
256   1   25  AA AB AC AD AE BA BB BC BD BE CA CB CC CD CE DA DB DC DD
              DE EA EB EC ED EE
384   2  100  Af Ag Ah Aj Ak Am Ap Aq As Av Bf Bg Bh Bj Bk Bm Bp Bq Bs
              Bv fA fB fC fD fE Cf Cg Ch Cj Ck Cm Cp Cq Cs Cv gA gB gC
              gD gE hA hB hC hD hE Df Dg Dh Dj Dk Dm Dp Dq Ds Dv jA jB
              jC jD jE kA kB kC kD kE mA mB mC mD mE Ef Eg Eh Ej Ek Em
              Ep Eq Es Ev pA pB pC pD pE qA qB qC qD qE sA sB sC sD sE
              vA vB vC vD vE
448   3  100  Ai Al An Ao Ar At Au Aw Ax Ay Bi Bl Bn Bo Br Bt Bu Bw Bx
              By Ci Cl Cn Co Cr Ct Cu Cw Cx Cy iA iB iC iD iE Di Dl Dn
              Do Dr Dt Du Dw Dx Dy lA lB lC lD lE nA nB nC nD nE oA oB
              oC oD oE Ei El En Eo Er Et Eu Ew Ex Ey rA rB rC rD rE tA
              tB tC tD tE uA uB uC uD uE wA wB wC wD wE xA xB xC xD xE
              yA yB yC yD yE
480   4   50  Ae Ad Ac Ab Aa Be Bd Bc Bb Ba Ce Cd Cc Cb Ca De Dd Dc Db
              Da eA eB eC eD eE Ee Ed Ec Eb Ea dA dB dC dD dE cA cB cC
              cD cE bA bB bC bD bE aA aB aC aD aE
496   5   10  AN BN CN DN EN NA NB NC ND NE
576   4  100  ff fg fh fj fk fm fp fq fs fv gf gg gh gj gk gm gp gq gs
              gv hf hg hh hj hk hm hp hq hs hv jf jg jh jj jk jm jp jq
              js jv kf kg kh kj kk km kp kq ks kv mf mg mh mj mk mm mp
              mq ms mv pf pg ph pj pk pm pp pq ps pv qf qg qh qj qk qm
              qp qq qs qv sf sg sh sj sk sm sp sq ss sv vf vg vh vj vk
              vm vp vq vs vv
672   6  200  fi fl fn fo fr ft fu fw fx fy gi gl gn go gr gt gu gw gx
              gy hi hl hn ho hr ht hu hw hx hy if ig ih ij ik im ip iq
              is iv ji jl jn jo jr jt ju jw jx jy ki kl kn ko kr kt ku
              kw kx ky lf lg lh lj lk lm lp lq ls lv mi ml mn mo mr mt
              mu mw mx my nf ng nh nj nk nm np nq ns nv of og oh oj ok
              om op oq os ov pi pl pn po pr pt pu pw px py qi ql qn qo
              qr qt qu qw qx qy rf rg rh rj rk rm rp rq rs rv si sl sn
              so sr st su sw sx sy tf tg th tj tk tm tp tq tv uf ug
              uh uj uk um up uq us uv vi vl vn vo vr vt vu vw vx vy wf
              wg wh wj wk wm wp wq ws wv xf xg xh xj xk xm xp xq xs xv
              yf yg yh yj yk ym yp yq ys yv
720   8  100  fe fd fc fb fa ge gd gc gb ga he hd hc hb ha je jd jc jb
              ja ke kd kc kb ka me md mc mb ma ef eg eh ej ek em ep eq
              es ev pe pd pc pb pa qe qd qc qb qa se sd sc sb sa df dg
              dh dj dk dm dp dq ds dv ve vd vc vb va cf cg ch cj ck cm
              cp cq cs cv bf bg bh bj bk bm bp bq bs bv af ag ah aj ak
              am ap aq as av
744  10   20  fN gN hN jN kN mN pN qN sN vN Nf Ng Nh Nj Nk Nm Np Nq Ns
              Nv
784   9  100  ii il in io ir it iu iw ix iy li ll ln lo lr lt lu lw lx
              ly ni nl nn no nr nt nu nw nx ny oi ol on oo or ot ou ow
              ox oy ri rl rn ro rr rt ru rw rx ry ti tl tn to tr tt tu
              tw tx ty ui ul un uo ur ut uu uw ux uy wi wl wn wo wr wt
              wu ww wx wy xi xl xn xo xr xt xu xw xx xy yi yl yn yo yr
              yt yu yw yx yy
840  12  100  ie id ic ib ia le ld lc lb la ne nd nc nb na oe od oc ob
              oa ei el en eo er et eu ew ex ey re rd rc rb ra te td tc
              tb ta ue ud uc ub ua di dl dn do dr dt du dw dx dy we wd
              wc wb wa xe xd xc xb xa ci cl cn co cr ct cu cw cx cy ye
              yd yc yb ya bi bl bn bo br bt bu bw bx by ai al an ao ar
              at au aw ax ay
868  15   20  iN lN nN oN rN tN uN wN xN yN Ni Nl Nn No Nr Nt Nu Nw Nx
              Ny
900  16   25  ee ed ec eb ea de dd dc db da ce cd cc cb ca be bd bc bb
              ba ae ad ac ab aa
930  20   10  eN dN cN bN aN Ne Nd Nc Nb Na
961  25    1  NN
```

61

Some comments about wildcard alphabets

It should be apparent from the construction of the wildcards that they group into classes following the distribution of Pascal's Triangle:

```
n
1            1    1
2         1    2    1
3      1    3    3    1
4    1    4    6    4    1
5  1    5   10   10    5    1
```

and so on.

Thus, if the base alphabet has n characters, there will be $\binom{n}{k}$ wildcards which base-include k characters, that is have degree k. Note that the number of wildcards of degree d is the same as the number of wildcards of degree $n-d$.

The wildcard alphabets are interesting, but the fun really doesn't begin until there are at least four characters in the base alphabet. Such an alphabet is the smallest for which there are at least two (non-eigencharacter) wildcards that do *not* match each other. For example, in $\mathbf{A_{DNA}}$, none of the following are *true*:
S ≈ W
M ≈ K
Y ≈ R
Clearly no base character equals another, and hence their extensions do not match.

PART III: SOLVING THE SIGNATURE STRING PROBLEM

...the popular tales about bad magic are specially full of the idea that evil alters and destroys the personality. The black witch turns a child into a cat or a dog; the bad magician keeps the Prince captive in the form of a parrot, or the princess in the form of a hind; in the gardens of the evil spirits human beings are frozen into statues or tied to the earth as trees. In all such instinctive literature **the denial of identity is the very signature of Satan**. In that sense it is true that the true God is the God of things as they are – or, at least, as they were meant to be. ... this power of seeing that a tree is *there*, in spite of you and me; that it holds of God and its own treeishness, is of great importance just now in practical politics.

GKC ILN Nov 22 1913
CW29:588-9, emphasis added

Art is the signature of man.

GKC *The Everlasting Man* CW2:166

The following case study is a presentation of the "Signature String Problem" which was the major topic of my doctoral dissertation. When I tell non-technical people about my research, I usually say that I helped biologists find "fingerprints" for bacteria, or (if the person is into the classics) I may mention that I was applying the idea of hapax legomena to genetic sequences. I also like to recall the old cartoon version of *The Cat in the Hat* and its bizarre song about a searching method called "Calculatus Eliminatus" which (as it said) found a thing by finding out where it wasn't. Both things are true, and fascinating.

1. A Statement of the Problem

> ...it is the test of a good encyclopaedia that it does two rather different things at once. The man consulting it finds the thing he wants; he also finds how many thousand things there are that he does not want.
> GKC "Consulting the Encyclopedia" in *The Common Man*

As I explained in detail earlier...

When I was a grad student I walked down a hall of the Biology Department and met two researchers who were studying a collection of ribosomal RNA (rRNA) sequences for a number of different species of bacteria. They were trying to find portions which could aid in identifying the bacteria in an unknown sample.

At that meeting they showed me their collection of rRNA sequences: it was on paper, in one of the biggest loose-leaf binders I had ever seen. Each sequence was about 1500 bases long, and there were 473 of these, about 700,000 characters total.

Later I learned more about their purpose in studying this collection: to synthesize *probes* – short RNA sequences marked with a molecule that would glow under ultraviolet light. These probes would enable them to study the numbers and kinds of bacteria in environmental samples. Therefore, these probes might need to be of three kinds:

1) probes which indicated a particular species,
2) probes which indicated a group of species,
3) probes which indicated almost any kind of bacteria.

They hoped to take advantage of the rRNA collection in deciding how to make these probes, since the rRNA for each of those species were unique, and yet related species contain similar areas, moreover, there were other areas which were the same in almost all species. But their problem was how to distinguish the various *degrees of uniqueness* within that given collection of sequences.

Thus it was clear that these researchers actually had several similar problems, each of which would be useful in identifying bacteria. These problems were related in their theoretical characteristics, but they also had a Cat-in-the-Hat-like quality in that one did not know exactly what it was one was seeking, even though the thing sought for was right there in the given collection, if it existed at all. Note especially that these are not "classical" search problems wherein we wish to locate a given string within a collection: here, we do *not* know what it is we are looking for, though if it exists, it must be in the given collection.

There is one other detail which needs to be stated: the collection, being a collection of *real* experimental rRNA sequences, contained wildcards: roughly one of every eighty characters or more than one percent of the total data. Thus any solution had to take them into account.

As a general guide, the shortest sequences which satisfy the problem are preferred. Practical reasons urge the finding of a *variety* of such sequences, if they exist, since some will be more suitable for use in the actual experiment than others. Some of these practical considerations were:

(1) Whether the proposed signature was not "too long" – the practical range was from 12 to 25 bases.

(2) Whether the proposed signature was very similar to a portion of a different species. If it was too similar, another would be preferred.

(3) Whether the "melting point" for the sequence was suitable.

(4) Whether the signature required the use of wildcards. One (or perhaps two) might be permitted, depending on the situation, and providing the other characteristics were suitable.

1. The Individual Signature String Problem (ISSP)

We wish to find sequences in our collection which appear in a *single* given species, but not in any other species. Formally, we are given a finite set S of distinct strings

$$S = \{\sigma_1, \sigma_2, \ldots \sigma_{card(S)}\}$$

over an alphabet A.
For each string σ in S, we wish to find strings $\tau = signature(S, \sigma)$ such that
  1) τ is a substring of σ

and
  2) τ is *not* a substring for any string in $S - \{\sigma\}$.

2. The Group Signature String Problem (GSSP)

We wish to find sequences in our collection which appear in a given *group* of species, but not in any other species in the collection. Formally, we are given a finite set S of distinct strings

$$S = \{\sigma_1, \sigma_2, \ldots \sigma_{card(S)}\}$$

over an alphabet A, and a proper subset $G \subset S$.
We wish to find strings $\tau = signature(S,G)$ such that
  1) τ is a substring of every string $\sigma \in G$

and
  2) τ is *not* a substring for any string in $S - G$.

3. The Universal Signature String Problem (USSP)
We wish to find a sequence in our collection which appears in as many species as possible in the collection. Formally, we are given a set S of distinct strings

$$S = \{\sigma_1, \sigma_2, \ldots \sigma_{card(S)}\}$$

over an alphabet A.
We wish to find strings $\tau = signature(S)$ such that τ is a substring of the greatest possible number of strings $\sigma \in S$.

We should here note that these are problems of computer science, not of biology, and require the designing of appropriate algorithms, along with establishing that they are correct and efficient.

Once the signatures are found for the given data, the biologists must evaluate them for appropriateness in producing probes, since various biochemical and practical requirements are imposed.

Signatures are Extensible

Assume we have found a signature δ (an individual signature) for a string σ in the set S of given strings over an alphabet A, which means the string σ has the form

$$\sigma = \alpha \bullet \delta \bullet \beta$$

for some strings α, β, possibly empty, over the given alphabet A.

If $\operatorname{len}(\alpha) > 0$, then $\alpha = \omega \bullet a$ for some (possibly empty) string ω, and a in A.

But since δ is a signature for σ, it appears nowhere in S–{σ}, that is, in no other string of S besides σ.

Hence, the string $a \bullet \delta$ *also* does not appear in S–{σ}, which means this extended string $a \bullet \delta$ is *also* a signature for σ.

By the same argument, a signature may be extended on the right, that is when $\operatorname{len}(\beta) > 0$ and $\beta = b \bullet \psi$ for some (possibly empty) string ψ, and b in A. Moreover this may be done as many times as desired. (Of course that means every string is its own signature, since the given set is "sufficiently distinct" to begin with.)

That means we may lengthen a signature by extending it from its original string, and the extended form remains a signature.

This observation is useful: while the computational limitations in our programming experiments found signatures of relatively short length (that is, in the range of six to eight characters) from the then-available rRNA data, practical matters in experimental biology required that a synthesized sequence be in the range of 12 to 25 bases. As we have noted, it was both easy and formally correct to lengthen our proposed (computed) signatures.

We must also note that in the case of non-individual signatures (that is group or universal signatures), such an extension may *only* be done provided that the adjacent character is *identical* in every strings involved in the group. Formally, let δ be a signature for both strings σ and τ, that is:

$$\sigma = \alpha \bullet \delta \bullet \beta$$

and

$$\tau = \mu \bullet \delta \bullet \nu$$

for some strings α, β, μ, ν, possibly empty, over the given alphabet A.

Then, *provided that* $\operatorname{len}(\alpha) > 0$, then $\alpha = \omega \bullet a$ for some (possibly empty) string ω, and a in A, *and also* $\operatorname{len}(\mu) > 0$, with $\mu = \psi \bullet a$ for some (possibly empty) string ψ, and *the same a* in A, then the string $a \bullet \delta$ is also a signature for both σ and τ.

The argument works the same for extension on the right, and for multiple extensions. It also works for more than two strings, provided that the extending character is identical for all of them. (I will leave the fun of showing this formally to the reader; you ought to have at least a little homework.)

2. THE BRUTE-FORCE SOLUTION

Given a collection of strings, we wish to find portions of each which are unique (or relatively so) as we have stated above. This sort of "search" for something not known in advance but which can readily be identified if correct seems analogous to those algebraic methods of finding roots of an equation without directly solving the equation. For example, those methods which find approximations to roots of a complex equation by iteration. In order to solve our problem, we iterate through all substrings of the given collection, and organize them in order to determine their uniqueness.

The Brute-Force Algorithm

There is, of course, a very straightforward solution to the problem, known as the brute-force approach. We select a relatively small integer k, the fixed length we wish to investigate. Then we examine every string, starting at the first position: we propose the substring of length k as a possible signature, and verify its correctness against all other strings in the collection. If it is not found elsewhere, it is a signature for the current string, so we store or report it. If it is found, we advance to the next position in that string, and continue until we have checked all strings. Here is the pseudo-code. Note that we use the relation *matches* rather than *equals*, thus this code works for both standard strings as well as those with wildcards.

For each string σ in S
    For each substring λ of length k in σ

        For each string τ other than σ in S
            For each substring μ of length k in τ
                if λ *matches* μ then
                    goto FOUND_ELSEWHERE
            Endfor ;;substring μ
        Endfor ;;string τ

        ;; here, substring λ does NOT appear elsewhere

        Report λ as a signature for σ.

FOUND_ELSEWHERE:
    ;; continue to next possible substring

    Endfor ;;substring λ
Endfor ;;string σ

This method works fine, and readily handles wildcards without difficulties, but it is quadratic in the number of characters. It is easily revised to report on every sort of signature encountered, simply by keeping a "score" on which strings contain a given substring: this score determines the "individuality" of that substring.

Here is the result for a simple example over the standard lower-case letters:

```
Strings:
  0   abcde
  1   cdpqrab
  2   abcpqf

ab      universal
bc      group    2:   0 2
cd      group    2:   0 1
de      individual 0
cd      group    2:   0 1
dp      individual 1
pq      group    2:   1 2
qr      individual 1
ra      individual 1
ab      universal
ab      universal
bc      group    2:   0 2
cp      individual 2
pq      group    2:   1 2
qf      individual 2
```

We studied two other methods which are more efficient, though more complex to implement. The first is a simple variation of the classic radix-sort, and it is able to handle strings over a wildcard alphabet. The second uses a sophisticated data structure called the "complete inverted file," which, with appropriate extensions, directly determines the signatures. It also can be adapted to handle wildcard strings.

3. The Radix-Sort Solution

This straightforward technique works in roughly linear time in the number of characters. It is a simple extension of the classic radix-sort approach, where substrings of a fixed length k are sorted into bucket-lists; each list is sorted by which string is referenced. Then, any bucket which has only one entry is a signature for that string. Furthermore, group signatures are found in those buckets in which the contents match the desired group. This requires in effect a single pass over the input data, though each character is considered k times.

This method is particularly efficient when the radix is computed by a idempotent hash function,[68] that is, in which the hash function $hash(\sigma) = \sigma$. This is possible when both the underlying alphabet and the desired length are "not too large." To be explicit, let n be the size of the alphabet A, $n = card(A)$, and k be the desired length of the signatures. Then when the product $n \cdot k$ is less than or equal to the word-size of the computer in bits, there is an easy and efficient solution. (The algorithm can, of course, be applied to arbitrary alphabets and lengths, but the implementation is not as tidy.)

For example, considering strings of DNA or RNA with a four-base alphabet, we need only two bits for each base[69] and so may readily find signatures of length 6 with a bucket-list of $4^6 = 2^{12} = 4096$ entries. That is, the strings may be represented in the following manner:

```
string      binary                    hex
AAAAAA      00 00 00 00 00 00         000
CAAAAA      01 00 00 00 00 00         400
GAAAAA      10 00 00 00 00 00         800
TAAAAA      11 00 00 00 00 00         c00
ACAAAA      00 01 00 00 00 00         100
CCAAAA      01 01 00 00 00 00         500
GCAAAA      10 01 00 00 00 00         900
TCAAAA      11 01 00 00 00 00         d00
AGAAAA      00 10 00 00 00 00         200
ATAAAA      00 11 00 00 00 00         300
AACAAA      00 00 01 00 00 00         040
AAGAAA      00 00 10 00 00 00         080
AATAAA      00 00 11 00 00 00         0c0
AAACAA      00 00 00 01 00 00         010
AAAGAA      00 00 00 10 00 00         020
AAATAA      00 00 00 11 00 00         030
AAAACA      00 00 00 00 01 00         004
AAAAGA      00 00 00 00 10 00         008
AAAATA      00 00 00 00 11 00         00c
AAAAAC      00 00 00 00 00 01         001
CCCCCC      01 01 01 01 01 01         555
AAAAAG      00 00 00 00 00 10         002
```

---

[68] Other hash functions (and other methods) may be used, depending on the demands of the particular situation.

[69] I prefer to use this mapping: $00_2 = 0 \rightarrow A$, $01_2 = 1 \rightarrow C$, $10_2 = 2 \rightarrow G$, $11_2 = 3 \rightarrow T$, as it is in alphabetical order. It also gives the Watson-Crick pairs (A with T, C with G) as Boolean complements: $\sim A \rightarrow \sim 00_2 = 11_2 \rightarrow T$, and $\sim C \rightarrow \sim 01_2 = 10_2 \rightarrow G$.

```
GGGGGG      10 10 10 10 10 10      aaa
AAAAAT      00 00 00 00 00 11      00c
TTTTTT      11 11 11 11 11 11      fff
```

Note that this is just one possible representation; the programmer may choose another mapping, or may reverse "endian" form, that is, the significance of the left and right ends.

Any six-character string over A_{DNA} may readily be converted to such a 12-bit integer (between 0 and 4095) by the following algorithm, or an equivalent:

```
Procedure ConvertDNAToIndex
argument
        in len
        in character array s
        returns integer
local
        integer i, index
begin
        index ← 0
        for 0 ≤ i < len
                index ← index SHIFT-LEFT 1
                select s[i]
                        case 'a': index ← index + 0
                        case 'c': index ← index + 1
                        case 'g': index ← index + 2
                        case 't': index ← index + 3
                endselect
        endfor
        return index
endproc
```

Here is the pseudo-code for the radix-sort method for a given length *k*:

Create the array of bucket-list headers of dimension 2^{2k}. (For *k*=6, there will be 2^{12}=4096 buckets.) These lists will be pairs <*s*,*p*> where *s* is which string in S, the input data, and *p* is the starting position of a *k*-character substring in that string.

```
Clear all buckets
For 0 ≤ i < card(S)
        ;; we consider each string σᵢ in S
        For 0 ≤ j ≤ len(σᵢ)–k
                ;; we examine each substring σᵢ of length k
                index ← ConvertDNAToIndex(k,σᵢ[j..j+k–1])
                ;; add that substring to the appropriate bucket
                Append [i,j] to bucket[index]
        Endfor ;; j
Endfor ;; i
```

A sample output for $k=3$, showing the bucket-index (in hex) for each of the substrings. The bucket report at the end shows only non-empty buckets; the entries show pairs $p:q$ where p is the string-index, and q the position in that string.

```
signature length 3 will have 64 buckets
Strings:
 0 acgtactta
 1 cttgagacg
 2 gagaacgtc

0 acgtactta
      0  acg  006
      1  cgt  01b
      2  gta  02c
      3  tac  031
      4  act  007
      5  ctt  01f
      6  tta  03c

1 cttgagacg
      0  ctt  01f
      1  ttg  03e
      2  tga  038
      3  gag  022
      4  aga  008
      5  gac  021
      6  acg  006

2 gagaacgtc
      0  gag  022
      1  aga  008
      2  gaa  020
      3  aac  001
      4  acg  006
      5  cgt  01b
      6  gtc  02d

Buckets:

001:  aac    2:3
006:  acg    2:4  1:6  0:0
007:  act    0:4
008:  aga    2:1  1:4
01b:  cgt    2:5  0:1
01f:  ctt    1:0  0:5
020:  gaa    2:2
021:  gac    1:5
022:  gag    2:0  1:3
02c:  gta    0:2
02d:  gtc    2:6
031:  tac    0:3
038:  tga    1:2
03c:  tta    0:6
03e:  ttg    1:1
```

As can readily be seen from the buckets, this simple example has signatures for each string, for each pair and a "universal" signature.

Radix-sort and Wildcards

When the strings have wildcards, we must adjust the algorithm in this manner: instead of computing the index for the k-character substring, we generate all eigenstrings which are included by that substring, and handle each of them as if they appeared at that position. That is, the contents of the inner loop are replaced with this code:

;; examine each substring σ_i of length k
;; expanding all wildcards to the included eigenstrings
For every eigenstring δ included by $\sigma_i[j$ for $k]$
    $index \leftarrow$ ConvertDNAToIndex(k,δ)
    ;; add that substring to the appropriate bucket
    Append $[i,j]$ to bucket[$index$]
Endfor ;; eigenstring δ

The code for such a loop is interesting to devise; I used a recursive approach to expand all included eigenstrings from a wildcard substring of length k.

Here is a sample output using wildcards. Observe that the list of three-character substrings shown below each of the originals are the eigenstrings included by the corresponding substring in the original. For example, in string 0, "abg" gives rise to "acg" and "agg" and "atg" all at position 0.

```
signature length 3 will have 64 buckets
Strings:
 0 abgtactta
 1 cttgmgacg
 2 gagaacgsc

0 abgtactta
     0 acg 006
     0 agg 00a
     0 atg 00ef
     1 cgt 01b
     1 ggt 02b
     1 tgt 03b
     2 gta 02c
     3 tac 031
     4 act 007
     5 ctt 01f
     6 tta 03c

1 cttgmgacg
     0 ctt 01f
     1 ttg 03e
     2 tga 038
     2 tgc 039
     3 gag 022
     3 gcg 026
     4 aga 008
     4 cga 018
     5 gac 021
     6 acg 006

2 gagaacgsc
     0 gag 022
     1 aga 008
     2 gaa 020
     3 aac 001
     4 acg 006
     5 cgc 019
     5 cgg 01a
     6 gcc 025
     6 ggc 029
```

```
Buckets:

001: aac   2:3
006: acg   2:4 1:6 0:0
007: act   0:4
008: aga   2:1 1:4
00a: agg   0:0
00e: atg   0:0
018: cga   1:4
019: cgc   2:5
01a: cgg   2:5
01b: cgt   0:1
01f: ctt   1:0 0:5
020: gaa   2:2
021: gac   1:5
022: gag   2:0 1:3
025: gcc   2:6
026: gcg   1:3
029: ggc   2:6
02b: ggt   0:1
02c: gta   0:2
031: tac   0:3
038: tga   1:2
039: tgc   1:2
03b: tgt   0:1
03c: tta   0:6
03e: ttg   1:1
```

Here again we can readily find the various kinds of signatures (individual, group, or universal) by examining the contents of the buckets.

4. THE COMPLETE INVERTED FILE SOLUTION

This method relies on the interesting data structure called the "complete inverted file" (CIF) the work of Blumer *et al.*[70] The CIF is an extension of the "directed acyclic word graph" or DAWG, which is itself an extension of simpler forms of graph-theoretic representations of strings such as the *trie* and PATRICIA. The Blumer algorithm to build the CIF for a given set of strings runs in time linear to the number of characters, and requires linear space as well. (We shall give details on both.)

In order to determine signatures, the CIF data structure is extended to indicate the uniqueness of the substring at a given node. The extensions to the algorithm also run in linear time, and require only modest additions to the main data structures.

The computation may also be done on strings with wildcards, though these must be handled as mentioned in the radix-sort technique, by adding each of the included eigenstrings.

Here is a brief overview of the Blumer algorithm to compute the DAWG and the CIF from a given set of strings. The pseudo-code is in Appendix 3.

We are given a set S of strings over a fixed finite base alphabet A. . The Blumer approach is a standard inductive strategy: knowing the DAWG for a set of strings and a prefix of length d of one additional string, we determine the new DAWG for those strings and the prefix of length (d+1) in constant time. Thus we can build the DAWG in linear time. This is accomplished by Phase 1 of the Blumer algorithm.

Once the DAWG is constructed, we annotate it with additional information (Phases 2 and 3, also done in linear time). This information enables us to construct the CIF in linear time. This is done by Phase 4.

Finally we annotate the CIF with further information (Phases 5, 6a, 6b), which enables the determination of signatures (Phase 7).

The algorithm first builds the corresponding DAWG (Phase 1) then executes four additional phases to compute the ident list (Phase 2) and implication pointer and length, (Phase 3) then revise the data structure to form the CIF (Phase 4) and compute the frequency count (Phase 5).

Blumer phase 1 This phase builds the DAWG from S, the input set of strings. Each string is scanned from left to right, inserting one character at a time into the presently existing DAWG, resulting in a new larger DAWG.

---

[70] Blumer, A., Blumer, J., Haussler, D., McConnell, R., and Ehrenfeucht, A. Complete inverted files for efficient text retrieval. *JACM* 34, 3 (1987) 578-595. For a review of antecedents, see Stephen, G. A. *String Search*. Technical Report TR-92-gas-01, School of Electronic Engineering Science, University College of North Wales (1992). The problem's history includes the 1960 *trie* of Fredkin, Morrison's *PATRICIA* data structure, the compact position trees of Weiner, suffix trees of McCreight; and directed acyclic word graphs (DAWGs) by Blumer *et al.* in the early 1980s.

Blumer phase 2 We build the **ident** lists: for each string in S, we start at its entry in the final array built in phase 1, and go up the chain of suffix pointers until we reach the source, adding the string id to each node reached.

Blumer phase 3 We use a depth-first traversal of the DAWG to set the **implication pointer** and **length** for all nodes.

Blumer phase 4 We perform a depth-first traversal to find the prime subwords in the DAWG, which are the nodes of the CIF, and determine their edges and labels.

Blumer phase 5 We perform a depth-first traversal of the CIF, computing the **frequency count** for each node.

After the Blumer phases are completed, the CIF is augmented with the uniset and kernel fields which enable the determination of signatures.

Phase 6a Using a depth-first traversal, we build the topological list of the CIF nodes (by setting the **topolink** pointer) and also compute **uniset**.

Phase 6b Using the result of phase 6a, traversethe CIF in forward topological order to compute the **kernel** for each node.

Phase 7 We perform another linear traversal of the CIF, using the **kernel** and **uniset** to determine the *minimal-length* signatures.
At each node a, examine each edge (a,b) labelled i
    If (1) the uniset of b has one member, and
        (2) the suffix of a is not NULL, and
        (3) the edge labelled i leaving the suffix of a
           goes to some node c which is not equal to b, and
        (4) uniset(c) is not equal to uniset(b),
then the string formed from the kernel of a followed by the first character of label(a,b) is a *signature* for the string identified by the label(a,b).

An Example

On the following pages we show the DAWG and CIF in both graphical and tabular form for the set S = {GGCUAACU, AGCUAACG, AAACUAAA}.

The Directed Acyclic Word Graph for
S = {GGCUAACU, AGCUAACG, AAACUAAA}

N	Sfx	Edges			implic ptr:len	i	e	k	label	ident
1	NIL	A→8	C→10 G→2 u→12		prime	0	0	0	ε	[3,2,1]
2	1		C→15 G→3		prime	1	1	1	G	[2]
3	2		C→4			(11:6)	1	2	2	GG
4	15			U→5	(11:5)	1	3	3	GGC
5	17	A→6			(11:4)	1	4	4	GGCU
6	19	A→7			(11:3)	1	5	5	GGCUA
7	21		C→9		(11:2)	1	6	6	GGCUAA
8	1	A→25	c→28 G→13		prime	1	5	1	A	[3]
9	23			U→11	(11:1)	1	7	7	GGCUAAC
10	1		g→24 U→12		prime	1	3	1	C	
11	30				prime	1	8	8	GGCUAACU	[1]
12	1	A→32			prime	1	4	2	CU	[1]
13	2		C→14		(24:6)	2	2	2	AG	
14	15			U→16	(24:5)	2	3	3	AGC	
15	10			U→17	(23:4)	1	3	2	GC	
16	17	A→18			(24:4)	2	4	4	AGCU	
17	12	A→19			(23:3)	1	4	3	GCU	
18	19	A→20			(24:3)	2	5	5	AGCUA	
19	32	A→21			(23:2)	1	5	4	GCUA	
20	21		C→22		(24:2)	2	6	6	AGCUAA	
21	3z4		C→23		(23:1)	1	6	5	GCUAA	
22	23		G→24		(24:1)	2	7	7	AGCUAAC	
23	28		g→24 u→11		prime	1	7	6	GCUAAC	
24	2				prime	2	8	8	AGCUAACG	[2]
25	8	A→26 C→28			prime	1	6	2	AA	[3]
26	25		C→27		prime	3	3	3	AAA	[3]
27	28			U→29	(35:4)	3	4	4	AAAC	
28	10		g→24 U→30		prime	1	7	3	AAC	
29	30	A→31			(35:3)	3	5	5	AAACU	
30	12	a→31			prime	1	8	4	AACU	[1]
31	32	A→33			(35:2)	3	6	6	AAACUA	
32	8	A→34			(34:1)	1	5	3	CUA	
33	34	A→35			35:1)	3	7	7	AAACUAA	
34	25	a→35 c→23			prime	1	6	4	CUAA	
35	26				prime	3	8	8	AAACUAAA	[3]

From left to right, the column headings are: **N** is the node number. **Sfx** is the suffix node number for that node. **Edges** are the edges leaving this node. For example, in node 1, "A→8" means there is an edge from node 1 to node 8 labelled "A." If the letter is uppercase, the edge is "primary" else it is "secondary" (as detailed in the Blumer paper). **implic** is either "**prime**" if the node's label is prime, or **(ptr:len)**, the implication values, where **ptr** is the implication pointer and **len** is the implication length. **label** is the label of the node, stored in (i,e,k): **i** is the string id of the label (i-th string in S); **e** is the end position of the label in that string; **k** is the length of the label in that string. **ident** is the list of string ids having the given label as a suffix.

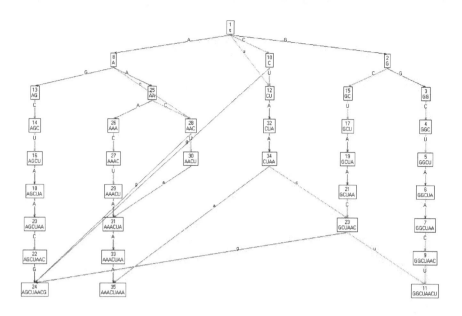

DAWG for {GGCUAACU, AGCUAACG, AAACUAAA}

The Complete Inverted File for
S = {GGCUAACU, AGCUAACG, AAACUAAA}

N	Sfx	s	e	k	us	fq	label	ident	edges
1	NIL	0	0	0	0	27		[3,2,1]	A→8 C→10 G→2 U→12
2	1	1	1	1	0	4	G	[2]	CUAAC→23 GCUAACU→11
8	1	1	5	1	0	11	A	[3]	A→25 C→28 GCUAACG→24
10	1	1	3	1	0	5	C		G→24 U→12
11	30	1	8	8	1	1	GGC<u>UAACU</u>	[1]	
12	1	1	4	2	0	4	C<u>U</u>	[1]	AA→34
23	28	1	7	6	0	2	GC<u>UAAC</u>		G→24 U→11
24	2	2	8	8	2	1	AGCUAA<u>CG</u>	[2]	
25	8	1	6	2	0	6	AA	[3]	A→26 C→28
26	25	3	3	3	3	2	AAA	[3]	CUAAA→35
28	10	1	7	3	0	3	A<u>AC</u>		G→24 U→30
30	12	1	8	4	0	2	A<u>ACU</u>	[1]	AAA→35
34	25	1	6	4	0	3	C<u>UAA</u>		A→35 C→23
35	26	3	8	8	3	1	AAAC<u>UAAA</u>	[3]	

From left to right, the column headings are: **N** is the node index. **Sfx** is the suffix pointer for that node. The label (s, e, k) for this node contains **s** the string id, **e** the end position, and **k**, the length of the label. **us** is the reduced uniset for N. **fq** is the frequency for N. **label** is the label of that node with the kernel <u>underlined</u>. **ident** is the ident list for that node. **edges** are the edges of the CIF. These have the form A→8 (in node 1) meaning an edge from 1 to 8 labelled A.

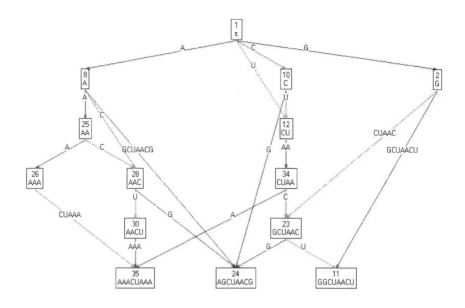

CIF for {GGCUAACU, AGCUAACG, AAACUAAA}

Finally, we show the signatures obtained from the above CIF.

N	label	edge	ker	s	sp	ln	sig
2	G	g	1	1	1	2	GG
8	A	g	1	2	1	2	AG
10	C	g	1	2	7	2	CG
23	GCUAAC	u	4	1	4	5	UAACU
25	AA	a	2	3	1	3	AAA
30	AACU	a	3	3	3	4	ACUA

From left to right, the column headings are: **N** is the CIF node index, **label** is its label, **edge** is the edge being considered, **ker** is the length of the kernel of that label. Then come three values indicating the signature: **s** is the source string, **sp** its starting point, and **ln** its length; **sig** is the signature string itself. Note that these signatures are *minimal*: no shorter substring may be found in the given data which remains a signature. Thus we have the following results:

original string	signatures
GGCUAACU	GG, UAACU
AGCUAACG	AG, CG
AAACUAAA	AAA, ACUA

PART IV: THE KMP ALGORITHM FOR WILDCARD ALPHABETS

In this section we examine the well-known Knuth-Morris-Pratt algorithm for string searching as applied to strings over wildcard alphabets. We will see that a naive attempt at applying the algorithm directly to such strings can yield erroneous results, and we set forth exactly why this occurs. Then we propose an extended form of the algorithm which handles such strings which maintains the efficiency of the original.

1. A Statement of the Problem

As discussed earlier, my doctoral work aided molecular biologists with their studies of rRNA sequences. At an early stage I devised a TOOL, a simple kind of "DNA spreadsheet" which assisted the biologists to explore those sequences on a computer. Its simple user interface enabled them to select a number of sequences for display and comparison, and it could perform some other simple analyses.

One operation was the simple "find this string" task, which accomplished by the usual "brute-force" $O(q \cdot d)$ algorithm wherein one slides the sought-for query string (of length q), character by character, past the entire data collection (containing d characters). This brute-force algorithm is easily and correctly extensible to handle strings which contain wildcards.

In the interests of speed, I changed the program to use the Knuth-Morris-Pratt (KMP) string search algorithm. This classic algorithm is examined in many standard algorithms texts such as Sedgewick's *Algorithms*. It builds a miniature Finite State Automaton based on the query string, and runs the data string through this, watching for a recognition of the search string; this takes $O(d)$ time. The KMP algorithm requires a character comparison relying on the standard equality of characters, in order to check whether a given character is identical to another, and it seemed reasonable[71] to simply replace that test with the weaker "matches" relation for wildcards.

However, I was surprised when the biologists informed me that my implementation was not working correctly. They tried to search for the string "GUCGUC" within the collection, and though the 16S rRNA sequence for the species *Eikenella corrodens* (str. FCD 373) contains the sequence "...NNUCGUC..." which clearly matches:

```
data      ...NNUCGUC...
search       GUCGUC
```

But my implementation of KMP *failed* to report the match. Fascinating.

I checked over the implementation, which I had tested with strings over the base alphabet, and it appeared to be correct. At that time, I did not pursue the matter further, as the particular question of extending the KMP to handle wildcard strings was not directly necessary to the signature string problems I was investigating. I merely changed back to the brute-force method and deferred further exploration of the matter. It was not until relatively recently, at the urging of a friend,[72] that I picked up the question again, located the difficulty, and formulated an alternative solution.

Finding the difficulty required a careful tracing through the algorithm. As you will see in the following chapter, the problem arises because the *matches* relation over wildcard alphabets is *not* transitive, and the KMP algorithm is relying upon the transitivity of the "equals" character-comparison test.

Devising an alternative was a good deal more intricate, but since the underlying scheme of the KMP algorithm is based upon Finite State Automata,

---

[71] In retrospect I should have investigated this assumption, but that's why I present this as a Case Study. It's good to recall what Chesterton said about this sort of thing: "There is no better test of a man's ultimate chivalry and integrity than how he behaves when he is wrong..." GKC, "The Real Dr. Johnson" in *The Common Man*, 120-1.

[72] My thanks to Dr. Chris Miller for urging me to complete the investigation.

and a wildcard is itself simply a miniature finite state automaton, it seemed reasonable to find a solution. The method is presented in the next chapter of this section; it is not terribly complex, and though it requires a bit more work than the KMP for base alphabets, it preserves the linear run-time complexity.

As a preliminary, we shall first present the "brute-force" algorithm, which we used as a check for our work. It is handy since it is simple and works for both base alphabets as well as for wildcard alphabets.

The Brute-Force Search Algorithm

This simple method locates a query string θ within a data string Δ. One simply slides θ, character by character, past the entire collection Δ, checking at each position whether the query "matches" the data at that position. When the strings are over a base alphabet, the function denoted below as "charcompare" is simply a test for equality of the arguments; when the strings are over a wildcard alphabet, the comparison may be the *matches* relation defined earlier, in which a bitwise AND is performed, and the result tested against zero: any non-zero result means that the two wildcards match (both base-include at least one character from the base alphabet).

```
Procedure BruteForceSearch
argument
        in character array query
        in character array data
        returns integer ;; (0 if not found, otherwise starting position in data)
local
        integer i, j
        boolean same
begin
        i ← 1
        repeat
                ;; (compare the query against the data starting at i)
                j ← 0
                same ← true
                repeat
                        if not charcompare(query[j+1], data[i+j]) then
                                same ← false
                        endif
                        j ← j+1
                until j > len(query)
                if same then
                        ;; (they match at position i)
                        return i
                endif
                i ← i+1
        until i > len(data) − len(query) + 1
        return 0
endproc
```

This common algorithm runs in $O(q \cdot d)$ time, and its examination along with improvements and discussion can be found in most algorithms texts.

The charcompare function

The function charcompare simply tests its two arguments and decides whether they are "equal" or not. In the usual implementation, charcompare will be something like this:

```
procedure charcompare (the classical form)
argument
   in character a,b ;; (over the base alphabet native to the computer)
returns
   boolean ;; (true if a equals b, else false)
begin
   if a = b then
           return true
   else
           return false
   endif
endproc
```

There are valid implementation reasons for generalizing this test to an explicit function, such as when one wants to handle case-insensitivity (enabling "E" to be equal to "e") or to ignore diacritical marks (enabling "é" or "ĕ" to be equal to "e") and so on.

In order to handle strings over the wildcard alphabet, we merely replace the strict equality with the weaker "matches" of the wildcard alphabet, in which case the function looks like this:

```
procedure charcompare (for wildcards)
argument
   in character a, b
           ;; (these arguments are characters in a WILDCARD alphabet
           ;; for which the base alphabet has at most bitsize(character) bits)
returns
   boolean ;; (true if a matches b, else false)
begin
   if (a BITWISE-AND b) ≠ 0 then
           return true
   else
           return false
   endif
endproc
```

This works correctly, as one can readily determine. However, applying this trick to the KMP algorithm will not work, as we shall now demonstrate.

2. A Naive Application of KMP to Wildcard Strings

There are two parts to this chapter. First we will review the original KMP algorithm. Then we analyze the difficulties which arise when it is naively made to handle a wildcard alphabet.

A Review of the Algorithm

This classic algorithm is examined in many texts such as Sedgewick's *Algorithms*. It locates a query string θ within a data string Δ. It is performed in two stages:

Preparation Stage: a finite state machine (in a special reduced form) is built which will recognize the query string. The data string plays no role in this computation, hence, the work accomplished in this stage may be used to check any number of data strings. The time is linear in the length of the query string $len(\theta)$, and requires additional memory of the same measure $len(\theta)$ for the storage of the automaton.

Search Stage: the data string is run through the automaton built in the Preparation Stage, and each recognition is returned. The time required is linear in the size of the data string, $len(\Delta)$.

Following is the pseudocode for the two stages, modified from Sedgewick's *Algorithms*.

```
Procedure KMPprep
argument
        in character array query
        out integer array next
local
        integer i,j
begin
        i ← 1
        j ← 0
        next[i]=0
        repeat
                if j=0 OR charcompare(query[i],query[j]) then
                        i ←   i + 1
                        j ←   j + 1
                        ;; (here, the first j+1 characters in query are the same as
                        ;; the LAST j+1 characters of its first i–1 characters)
                        next[i] ← j
                else
                        j ← next[j]
                endif
        until i > len(query)
endproc
```

```
Procedure KMPsearch
    argument
        in character array data
        in character array query
        in integer array next ;; (previously computed by KMPprep)
    returns
        integer
        ;; (returns the location in data where query was found,
        ;; if greater than len(data), it was not found.)
    local
        integer i,j
    begin
1       i ← 1
2       j ← 1

3       repeat
4           if j=0 OR charcompare(data[i],query[j]) then
5               i ← i + 1
6               j ← j + 1
7           else
8               j ← next[j]
9           endif
10      until j > len(query) OR i > len(data)

11      if j > len(query) then
12          return i – len(query)
13      else
14          return i
    endproc
```

Failure of the original KMP as naively applied to wildcards

We now show how the naive extension of KMP which performs "match" (rather than equality) gives a faulty result when applied to a data string with wildcards.

Consider the following:
   $data$ = "NNTC"
   $query$ = "GTC"

Clearly, the query string matches the data string beginning at the second character. Moreover, we note that the query string contains *no* wildcards, so there are no doubts about the correctness of the results produced by KMPprep.

Let us, then, step through KMPsearch and see what happens.

line	i	j	data[i]	query[j]	comment
3	1	1	N	G	first entry of the loop
4	1	1	N	G	charcompare returns **true**, take then-branch
5,6	2	2	N	T	increment the pointers
9,10	2	2	N	T	termination not met, loop again
4	2	2	N	T	charcompare returns **true**, take then-branch
5,6	3	3	T	C	increment the pointers
9,10	3	3	T	C	termination not met, loop again
4 (ERROR)	3	3	T	C	charcompare returns **false**, take else-branch
8	3	1	T	G	advance *j* by its entry in *next*
9,10	3	1	T	G	termination not met, loop again
4	3	1	T	G	charcompare returns **false**, take else-branch

8	3	0	T	?	advance *j* by its entry in *next*
9,10	3	0	T	?	termination not met, loop again
4	3	0	T	?	*j* is zero, take then-branch
5,6	4	1	C	G	increment the pointers
9,10	4	1	C	G	termination not met, loop again
4	4	1	C	G	charcompare returns **false**, take else-branch
8	4	0	C	?	advance *j* by its entry in *next*
9,10	4	0	C	?	termination not met, loop again
4	4	0	C	?	*j* is zero, take then-branch
5,6	5	1	?	G	increment the pointers
9,10	5	1	?	G	termination met, exit loop
11	5	1	?	G	1 not less than 3, take else-branch
13,14	5	1	?	G	returns 5 as result: query does not appear in data

So this "implementation" of KMP for wildcards does not perform correctly. We can see the mistake happening (where "ERROR" appears above) but why does it happen?

The brief answer is because the *matches* relation is not transitive. But this sounds obscure; it is a strange sort of answer, since there does not seem to be any sort of transitivity going on in the algorithm. However, the classic KMP algorithm is relying implicitly upon the fact that the usual charcompare function, naturally the *equals* relation of a base alphabet, is transitive. But let us spell this out in detail.

The algorithm goes wrong at the point marked "ERROR." Clearly, since charcompare("T","C") is **false**, the query "GTC" does not agree with the data at position 1. That much is correct, and we correctly take the else-branch of the if.

However, the advance specified by *next*[3] is too severe. The (accurate) disagreement of T and C should *not* mean to restart the comparison at position 1 of the query string with position 3 of the data, because GTC *does* in fact *match* at position 2 of the data.

So we ask, why is *next*[3] set to 1? Because when KMPprep examined the query string, the first character G was found to *not* equal the second character T. In strings over a base alphabet, it is not possible for a string which start with "GTx" where x is not "C" to be equal to "GTC" starting at the second position.

Why? Because of transitivity. Since Δ[2] = θ[2], but θ[2] ≠ θ[1], in must be true that Δ[2] ≠ θ[1]. Remember, in the classic algorithm, the strings are over the base alphabet which uses the *equals* relation, which is **transitive**: for a = b and b ≠ c, we must have a ≠ c.

In our example, the N at *data*[1] does *match* both G and T: in fact, *data*[2] matches *query*[2] and even though *query*[1] does not match *query*[1], it is true that *data*[2] matches *query*[1]. Or to be specific, although it is true that

N *matches* T (that is, *data*[1] versus *query*[2])

and

T *does not match* G (that is, *query*[2] versus *query*[1])

yet it is true that

N *matches* G. (that is, *data*[1] versus *query*[1]).

What is going on in *next*? This table is computed by KMPprep and indicates what to do when the query and the data disagree at a given position. This is examined in detail in typical algorithms texts[73] and the reasoning works like this:

If the first character in the data string is not equal to the first character of the query, there is nothing to "remember"; the position must be advanced, and the search begins again at the next position of the data string.

If (on the other hand) the first characters agree, that fact must be remembered, and the next characters compared. If they agree, fine; the search advances in both strings. But if they do not agree, the action depends on the situation relating the first with the second character of the query string: could there be a *new* appearance of the query within the data beginning at this position? That is, there could be an agreement (maybe only partial) of the data at both the first and the second position of the query. The *next* table tracks the possibilities with regard to the query string; it tells us how to advance correctly for the transitive *equals* relation of base alphabets, but the *next* table as computed by the above KMPprep algorithm cannot correctly handle the non-transitivity of the *matches* relation for wildcard strings.

Thus, when we naively altered the algorithm in an attempt to replace the *equals* relation (which *is* transitive) with the *matches* relation (which is *not* transitive), we introduced an error which was very subtle, relying upon a fundamental characteristic of the underlying algebra. In the usual situation, with strings over base alphabets using the *equals* relation (which is transitive) such a case can only occur when the query string starts with a repeated character. However, with strings over a wildcard alphabet, where the *matches* relation is not transitive, there are a variety of possibilities, some of which (as we have just seen) occur when there are wildcards in the data, even though there were none in the query.

We can, therefore, understand what went wrong with the naive implementation. Now let us see how to extend the KMP algorithm to handle wildcards.

---

[73] See e.g. Sedgewick, *Algorithms*, 244-9.

3. Extending KMP to Handle Wildcard Strings

As we explained earlier, the classic KMP algorithm builds a finite state automaton (FSA) which can recognize the query string. The data string is then scanned by that FSA, and each recognition is reported. Even without bothering with the issues relating to wildcard alphabets, it is clear that one can build the FSA for a query which contained "alternatives" (which are none other than our wildcard characters), just as one can build FSAs for any valid regular expression.[74]

States for the KMP wildcard FSA

In order to recognize a wildcard string, the states of the automaton must represent the *combinations* of matching prefixes within the query string. Then, as each character of the data string is considered, the automaton advances its state based on that character, and as in the classic algorithm for strings over a base alphabet, there is no need to back up in the data string.

In the classic algorithm, the state represents the length of the prefix of the query string which agrees (equals) at that position within θ, the query string. But in the extended form, the matches relation has the effect of permitting any given position in the query string to agree (be matched with) a *collection* of positions. So the state may be represented as a vector $\mathbf{s} = <s_1, s_2, ... s_{len(\theta)}>$ of $len(\theta)$ bits, representing a collection of prefixes: if a given element s_i is one, then the prefix of θ with length i is included in that state; s_i is zero if that prefix is not included.

Thus there are exactly $2^{len(\theta)}$ possible states for a given query string θ, though as we shall see, some query strings will not require all of them.

It is convenient to have routines to convert between this vector $\mathbf{s}$ and its corresponding index s, where $0 \leq s \leq 2^{len(\theta)}$.

To convert the vector form $\mathbf{s}$ of a state into its index, we define

$$\text{index}(\mathbf{s}) = \sum_{i=1}^{|\theta|} s_i \bullet 2^{i-1}$$

which can be implemented in this or similar pseudocode:

```
Procedure MakeIndex
argument
        in bit array state
        out integer index
local
        integer i
        integer powertwo
begin
        powertwo ← 1
        for 1 ≤ i ≤ querylength
                index ← index + powertwo*state[i]
                powertwo ← powertwo SHIFT-LEFT 1
        endfor
endproc
```

---

[74]Regular expressions (RE) and finite state automata (FSA) are interconvertible, being merely two variant representations of the same formal entity: a RE describes the strings as they appear; the FSA describes a mechanism by which such strings can be recognized or generated. See any text on automata theory.

And to convert the state index n with $0 \leq n \leq 2^{len(\theta)}$ into its corresponding vector, we define
$$vector(n) = \langle n_1, n_2, \ldots n_{len(\theta)} \rangle$$
where
$$n_i = \lfloor (n \bmod 2^i)/2^{i-1} \rfloor \text{ for } 1 \leq i \leq len(\theta).$$

Again taking advantage of the binary nature of computers, we can use something like this:

```
Procedure MakeVector
argument
        in integer index
        in integer querylength
        out bit array state
local
        integer i
begin
        for 1 ≤ i ≤ querylength
                state[i] ← index BIT-AND 1
                index ← index SHIFT-RIGHT 1
        endfor
endproc
```

Start state

The start state has index zero, the vector of all zeros, indicating that no prefix is matched.

Final states

The final state(s) are those for which the prefix is included which has the same length as the query string itself. These vectors have the last component $n_{len(\theta)}$ equal to one, or equivalently, have an index greater that or equal to $2^{len(\theta)-1}$.

```
Procedure IsFinalState
argument
  in integer stateindex
  in integer querysize
  return boolean
begin
  if stateindex ≥ (1 SHIFT-LEFT querysize) then
        return true
  else
        return false
  endif
endproc
```

Transitions

Transitions are specified by a function mapping a state and a character into a state:
$$T: state \times character \rightarrow state$$
In order to determine the destination state from a given state **s** (the "from-state") and character **a** in the wildcard alphabet, we must compute the effect that character

would have on each prefix in that given state when augmented by that character, which will determine the destination or "to-state."

Initially, we see whether the first character of the query string matches the given character **a**. If they match, then the destination state contains a prefix of length one; otherwise it does not. Then we advance through the query, checking whether the from-state contains that prefix and **a** matches the next character. Either we have a match, in which case the augmented prefix belongs to the destination state. Or, there is no match, in which case that prefix does not belong to the destination state.

The computation is specified by the following pseudocode:

```
Procedure ComputeWildcardTransition
argument
        in bit array FromState
        in wildchar ThisChar
        in wildchar array Query
        out bit array ToState
local
        integer i
begin
        if Matches(Query[1],ThisChar) then
                ToState[1]←1
        else
                ToState[1]←0
        endif

        For 2 ≤ i ≤ len(Query)
                If FromState[i–1] = 1 then
                        if Matches(Query[i],ThisChar) then
                                ToState[i]←1
                        else
                                ToState[i]←0
                        endif
                else
                        ToState[i]←0
                endif
        endfor
endproc
```

The first conditional checks whether the prefix of length one of the query matches the given character, and marks the to-state accordingly.

Then, the loop advances through the query string: the index i represents the current prefix length being considered. We check whether the prefix of one fewer characters is within the from-state, and if it is, we augment the prefix by *thischar*. If this augmented prefix matches the query, which is established by checking whether *thischar* matches the i-th character of the query string, then this prefix (of length i) belongs to the to-state; otherwise it does not belong.

Note that we require the from-state in order to compute the to-state (we always know the starting state which is all zero) but we only need compute any given state once: thus we advance from "unvisited" to "visited" states.

As will be seen from the following pseudocode, we chose to use a "visited" bit for each state, and a stack of unvisited states. The above-specified "vector" and "index" functions are trivial and omitted.

```
Procedure WildKMPprep
argument
    in wildchar array Query
    in wildchar array Alphabet
    out integer array State[2^{len(Query)},card(Alphabet)]
local
    stack Stack
    bit array Visited[2^{len(Query)}]
    integer fromstateindex
    integer queryindex
    wildchar thischar
    bit array fromstate[2^{len(Query)}]
    bit array tostate[2^{len(Query)}]
begin
    push 0 on Stack
    Visited[]←false
    while Stack not empty
        fromstateindex←pop Stack
        MakeVector(fromstateindex, len(Query), fromstate)
        Visited[fromstateindex] ←true

        for thischar in Alphabet
            ;; compute the transition for this fromstate and character
            ComputeWildcardTransition(fromstate,thischar,Query,tostate)

            ;; convert the vector version of tostate into an index
            MakeIndex(tostate,tostateindex)

            ;; record it in our table
            State[fromstate,thischar]=tostate

            ;; if we've not yet handled this state, put it on the stack
            if not Visited[tostate] then
                push tostate on Stack
            endif
        endfor ;; for every wildcard character
    endwhile ;; while stack isn't empty
endproc
```

The above algorithm does not look too appealing. Its run time is of order $len(\theta) \cdot 2^{len(\theta)} \cdot card(\mathbf{A})$, since there are $2^{len(\theta)} \cdot card(\mathbf{A})$ states, each of which require $len(\theta)$ checks of prefixes. However, queries are typically short, certainly far shorter than the data against which they are to be compared. Moreover, the above algorithm need only be performed once for any given query, and any number of data strings might be tested with the resulting FSA. Note also that space on the order of $2^{len(\theta)} \cdot card(\mathbf{A})$ is required for the state table.

The KMP algorithm for wildcards

Now we have our transition table for the FSA, and are able to use it to search for that query string. Fortunately, our FSA continues to function in linear time as in the classic KMP, and requires very little additional machinery.

```
Procedure WildKMPsearch
argument
    in integer Querylength
    in integer array State[2^Querylength, card(Alphabet)] (as computed above)
        in wildchar array Data
        out integer list Found
    local
        integer fromstate
        integer tostate
        integer i
    begin
        empty Found
        fromstate←0
        i←1
        while i ≤ len(Data)
            tostate←State[fromstate, Data[i]]
            if IsFinalState(tostate, Querylength) then
                ;; record that we've found the query at this position
                append i to Found

                ;;alternatively, if we only need the first occurrence,
                ;; we could return it here.
            endif

            ;; advance to the next state and data character
            fromstate ← tostate
            i ← i+1
        endwhile ;; for all the characters of the data
    endproc
```

Clearly, the above is linear in the length of the data, as in the classic KMP algorithm.

Some results

We implemented the above algorithms in order to study the actual performance. In particular we were curious to learn how many states are required by the KMP-search FSA for a given query string. Our testing was primarily aimed at strings over the (reduced) DNA wildcard alphabet, which contains 15 characters. (A "reduced" wildcard alphabet omits the null-match.)

Thus there are 15^4 possible queries of length 4, which is 50625.

For a query of length 4, there are 16 different states for the FSA, representing which of the four possible prefixes are being matched at a given point (any combination of 1, 2, 3, or 4 characters).

Example AAAA This query requires five states:
state 0: (start) no characters match.
state 1: prefix of length 1 matches
state 3: prefixes of length 1 and 2 match
state 7: prefixes of length 1, 2, and 3 match
state 15: (final) prefixes of length 1, 2, 3, and 4 match

The transitions are the following:

```
State 0 (start)
    on A M R V W H D N goto 1
    on C G S T Y K B   goto 0
State 1
    on A M R V W H D N goto 3
    on C G S T Y K B   goto 0
State 3
    on A M R V W H D N goto 7
    on C G S T Y K B   goto 0
State 7
    on A M R V W H D N goto 15
    on C G S T Y K B   goto 0
State 15 (final)
    on A M R V W H D N goto 15
    on C G S T Y K B   goto 0
```

Note that the wildcards A, M, R, V, W, H, D, N are those which *match* A; the others C, G, S, T, Y, K, B *do not* match A.

Example ACAM: This query requires 11 states, specifically:
state 0: (start) no characters match.
state 1: prefix of length 1 matches
state 2: prefix of length 2 matches
state 3: prefixes of lengths 1 and 2 match
state 5: prefixes of lengths 1 and 3 match
state 7: prefixes of lengths 1, 2, and 3 match
state 9: (final) prefixes of lengths 1 and 4 match
state 10: (final) prefixes of lengths 2 and 4 match
state 11: (final) prefixes of lengths 1, 2 and 4 match
state 13: (final) prefixes of lengths 1, 3 and 4 match
state 15: (final) prefixes of lengths 1, 2, 3, and 4 match

The FSA has the following transitions

```
State 0 (start)
 on A M R V W H D N goto 1
 on C G S T Y K B goto 0
State 1
 on A R W D goto 1
 on C S Y B goto 2
 on M V H N goto 3
 on G T K goto 0
```

```
State 2
 on A M R V W H D N goto 5
 on C G S T Y K B goto 0
State 3
 on A R W D goto 5
 on C S Y B goto 2
 on M V H N goto 7
 on G T K goto 0
State 5
 on A R W D goto 9
 on C S Y B goto 10
 on M V H N goto 11
 on G T K goto 0
State 7
 on A R W D goto 13
 on C S Y B goto 10
 on M V H N goto 15
 on G T K goto 0
State 9 (final)
 on A R W D goto 1
 on C S Y B goto 2
 on M V H N goto 3
 on G T K goto 0
State 10 (final)
 on A M R V W H D N goto 5
 on C G S T Y K B goto 0
State 11 (final)
 on A R W D goto 5
 on C S Y B goto 2
 on M V H N goto 7
 on G T K goto 0
State 13 (final)
 on A R W D goto 9
 on C S Y B goto 10
 on M V H N goto 11
 on G T K goto 0
State 15 (final)
 on A R W D goto 13
 on C S Y B goto 10
 on M V H N goto 15
 on G T K goto 0
```

We arranged our test program to generate all possible query strings of a given length, and compute the FSA by the above algorithm, recording the varieties of states used by each one. The result is tabulated below; there are 29 different classes of FSA considering the arrangements of necessary states, ranging from the minimum, 5, (which is one added to the length of the query), to the maximum, 16 (which is two raised to the length of the query). The table shows a sample query-string which results in that class of state arrangement

```
   total query states contained:
 1    369 AAAA    5   0 1 . 3 . . . 7 . . .  .  .  . 15
 2    496 MMAC    6   0 1 . 3 . . . 7 . . . 11  .  . 15
 3    304 MAAC    6   0 1 . 3 . . . 7 . 9 .  .  .  . 15
 4    160 AAAC    6   0 1 . 3 . . . 7 8 . .  .  .  . 15
 5    432 VMAG    7   0 1 . 3 . . . 7 . 9 . 11  .  . 15
 6    336 MMAG    7   0 1 . 3 . . . 7 8 . . 11  .  . 15
 7    336 MAAG    7   0 1 . 3 . . . 7 8 9 .  .  .  . 15
 8    736 MACA    7   0 1 . 3 . 5 . 7 . . . 11  .  . 15
 9    194 AAMA    7   0 1 . 3 4 . . 7 . 9 .  .  .  . 15
10    192 VMAT    8   0 1 . 3 . . . 7 8 9 . 11  .  . 15
11    302 AACA    8   0 1 . 3 4 . . 7 . 9 . 11  .  . 15
12    830 AMAA    8   0 1 2 3 . 5 . 7 . . . 11  .  . 15
13   2576 MACC    9   0 1 . 3 . 5 . 7 . 9 . 11  . 13 . 15
14    942 AACC    9   0 1 . 3 4 . . 7 8 9 .  . 12  . 15
15    528 MAGA    9   0 1 . 3 4 5 . 7 . 9 . 11  .  . 15
16   1794 ACAC    9   0 1 2 3 . 5 . 7 . . 10 11  .  . 15
17    288 MRAC    9   0 1 2 3 . 5 . 7 . 9 . 11  .  . 15
18   1248 MACG   10   0 1 . 3 . 5 . 7 8 9 . 11  . 13 . 15
19    962 AACM   10   0 1 . 3 4 . . 7 8 9 . 11 12  . 15
20   1248 MAGC   10   0 1 . 3 4 5 . 7 . 9 . 11  . 13 . 15
21   1154 ACAA   10   0 1 2 3 . 5 . 7 . 9 . 11  . 13 . 15
22    336 MRAS   10   0 1 2 3 . 5 . 7 . 9 10 11  .  . 15
23    528 AMAG   10   0 1 2 3 . 5 . 7 8 . 10 11  .  . 15
24   1406 ACAM   11   0 1 2 3 . 5 . 7 . 9 10 11  . 13 . 15
25    192 MRAT   11   0 1 2 3 . 5 . 7 8 9 10 11  .  . 15
26   3264 MAGG   12   0 1 . 3 4 5 . 7 8 9 . 11 12 13 . 15
27    912 ACAG   12   0 1 2 3 . 5 . 7 8 9 10 11  . 13 . 15
28   5168 ACCA   12   0 1 2 3 4 5 6 7 . 9 . 11  . 13 . 15
29  23392 ACCC   16   0 1 2 3 4 5 6 7 8 9 10 11 12 13 14 15
```

For a query length of three, there are 3375 possible query strings, divided into 6 classes as shown in the following table:

```
1    175 AAA 0000008b  4:  0 1 . 3 . . . 7
2    304 MAC 000000ab  5:  0 1 . 3 . 5 . 7
3    160 AAC 000000 9b  5:  0 1 . 3 4 . . 7
4    336 MAG 000000bb  6:  0 1 . 3 4 5 . 7
5    496 ACA 000000af  6:  0 1 2 3 . 5 . 7
6   1904 ACC 000000ff  8:  0 1 2 3 4 5 6 7
```

We also generated tables for queries of length 5 and 6, summarized as follows:

qlen	maxstrings	maxstates	classes	nmax	percent
2	225	4	2	160	71.1
3	3375	8	6	1904	56.4
4	50625	16	29	23392	46.2
5	759375	32	185	294464	38.8
6	11390625	64	1827	3775360	33.0

where:
$qlen$ is the length of the query string
$maxstrings = 15^{qlen}$, the total number of possible strings of that length over $\mathbf{A_{DNA}}$
$maxstates = 2^{qlen}$, the total possible states containing prefixes from 0 to $qlen$)
$classes$ is the number of distinct state sets used by the FSA for any query string
$nmax$ is the number of all query strings using the maximum number of states
$percent = 100 * nmax / maxstrings$.

PART V: SOME OTHER CASE STUDIES

> I write this article in a kind of crooked, half-country lane which, taking a turn at the bottom, opens upon the sea. Now I might walk down that lane a million times, and I should still feel that it was right to have walked down it a million times; that it was right to dwell in such a place and to be used to it. The lane is irregular, but it is not abrupt. The sea is awful, but it is not startling. It seems easy to accept the fact that they are always there; it is natural that Nature should be natural. But I know another lane in England crooked also, though a little broader round one corner, of which one sees something more splendid than the sea. The name of this lane is Fleet Street, and the sight is the dreadful dome and cross which Wren set in the sky. Now, when I see this, I do not feel that it is a thing meant to be seen a million times; but once or twice or thrice at some strange crisis of the soul. The sea lies in wait to soothe, but this lies in wait to amaze and to awaken. The sea is a lullaby; the church is an alarum. The waves beyond this little lane are waiting to tell me that Nature is patient and long-lived, and that we are secure in her bosom. But the Cathedral is waiting to tell me that we are not secure, that the sea can be upheaved and the earth be shaken, that heaven and earth shall pass away, but that words [of Christ] shall not pass away.
>
> GKC ILN Aug 31 1907 CW27:539-40

In collecting and examining my archives to arrange the foregoing studies, I found a few other items which will be of interest, even if they are not exactly relevant to those topics. Since a fairly large amount of my work in computing has been the manipulation of characters, as distinct from calculation in the mathematical sense, they can rightly be considered in this volume.

1. CASE STUDY: THE "AWAKENING"

In the first of my monographs on problem-solving, I related my first days at Frankel Engineering Labs (FEL), back in September of 1977: how there were two old HP2116 computers running a form of time-share BASIC. Users at various industries in or near Reading, Pennsylvania, used the telephone and "dialled in" to these machines, using FEL-written software to do engineering – primarily generating "part-programs" for use on numerically controlled machine tools – or the common tasks of data processing for business. Those were FEL's two departments: NC (numerical control) and DP (data processing), and while there were many occasions of intramural rivalry, we did have a lot of fun, especially when someone's birthday came around.

These two old HP machines were certainly satisfactory for that day and age.[75] They could only run an interpretive form of an early and non-sophisticated dialect of BASIC; this had *very* limited memory resources (about 5K for both program and working memory) and the disk files it supported were also limited in size and

---

[75] Of course they had limitations, just as our present-day machines do, though they were cutting-edge in comparison to the other machine, the old CDC 160 – this had 4096 words each of 12 bits, which were magnetic core, not solid-state; its only input and output was by paper-tape, and it had *no* external memory whatsoever! It had been purchased in 1960, and was still being used regularly when I started at FEL in 1977. I should note that it had been designed by Seymour Cray, and when I left FEL in 1983 it was still functional and still in use, 23 years after being installed. See the first Case Studies volume for more about it.

internal structure. Also the hardware itself was a hybrid of at least three different manufacturers: the large disk drives used for permanent memory were nearly as big as washing machines, and made almost as much noise, and despite careful daily servicing of the drive heads and magnetic platters, we had rather frequent disk errors. Moreover, the needs in both DP and NC departments demanded a more sophisticated system, a better and faster programming language, larger and better file storage – but in particular both we and our customers demanded a more reliable system.

As I recounted in the first volume, Samuel R. Frankel, the founder and owner and my boss, was a professional mechanical engineer, and in 1960 he bought a CDC 160, one of the first computers in the Reading area, for use in doing numerical approximations of difficult thermodynamics problems for a local steel company. He again did his homework, "due diligence" as it is now called, and decided on one of HP's new 3000-series "minicomputers." It ran a regular multi-user operating system, and supported FORTRAN and both interpretive and compiled BASIC as well as other languages; it had a data base integrated into its system, and it could handle much higher terminal speeds. It sounded splendid in so many ways...

There was just one major obstacle, overlooking the dull issues like cost, delivery, installation, getting used to it, and all the rest. The BASIC on that system was a good deal more sophisticated than the version we were using, but even more, there was no way of transporting any of our current programs or files over to that machine.

I know that this will astound many readers, so used to thinking of the INTERNET, and floppy disks, and thumb drives and so forth.[76] But in the late 1970s there were only two ways of transporting data between computers: magnetic tapes and paper-tapes. It was not reasonable to type in, punch onto paper-tape, or re-program all our existing software; besides, there was also a large amount of user data in files – active data, too – and this data had to be transported from the Old World of the HP 2116 machines to the New World of the HP 3000.

Fortunately, Sam and the others at FEL already knew that I was an inquisitive, daring, lunatic programmer who had a background in deeper things like the internal working of compilers and the representation of numbers. I also had some relevant experience in what is now called "reverse engineering":[77] I knew (from my explorations of the CDC 6400 during my undergraduate years) of utilities like "DMP" which printed the internal contents of working memory, and had learned how to perform disassembly and grasp the sense of the machine instructions... And so, when we discussed the question of how we were going to convert from the Old World to the New, I asked whether we could arrange to get a "dump" of one of our backup tapes. Sam took one of these to a local bank where he knew people in their data processing department, and they produced a printout of that tape's contents.

---

[76] Though floppy disks were around: as part of a completely separate project FEL was borrowing a small "desktop" machine from Olivetti which was an early sort of personal computer. It used two eight-inch floppys; there were no internal hard drives, and it had a built-in printer and a tiny one-line display, but no display screen.

[77] During my junior year at college, I had de-compiled a small utility written by one of the civil engineering professors and used by students taking the surveying course.

I now put on my Champollion[78] hat, and with a printed form of an actual BASIC program in one hand and the dump in the other, began "decoding" the internal representations used by the old systems to store the entire collection of permanently stored files: at the higher level, how those files were arranged on the tape, and then, at the lower level, how data was represented in data files, and how the elements of interpretive BASIC programs were stored in a program. This sounds a good deal harder than it was; there are not that many elements to the representation, as that old BASIC was a very simple dialect.

What I ended up with was exactly what was in the old BASIC interpreter: a routine which could take the internal representation and reconstitute (in printed form) the original source.

I ought to point out that this program was developed for the *new* system; we were given access to another machine for development of the process.

Once the hard part was done, I simply had to arrange that the re-generated file was stored, and ready for checking by the appropriate department. The data files were much easier, as they required only the translation of the floating-point numbers and strings from their Old World forms into those used by the New World.

We called the entire tool which resulted AWAKE, and the process was the Awakening. According to my records of that era, the new HP3000 system came on August 16, 1978, though it was not "up and running" until September 7. Once it was officially given over to us for use, I had to finish my work on Awake while the other departments began arranging the necessary accounting structures (both financial and system-related) for our customers.

Since the typical data processing customers were working on a day-to-day basis, the transition had to be properly coordinated, both from the computational side as well as the user side. And then, on Friday September 15, I did the first Awakening for one of our data processing customers, and the next week they were using the new system. Not only was it a more reliable system (though of course it also crashed once in a while), but they also had far faster throughput.

Over the next weeks and months, the rest of the customers were moved over, and eventually the two old HP2116s were shut off permanently.

---

[78] The French scholar who decyphered the Rosetta Stone, which had both Egyptian hieroglyphics and Greek along with another form of Egyptian known as Demotic.

2. Case Study: the "Micro" tool

As I mentioned, there were two departments at Frankel Engineering: DP (data processing) and NC (numerical control), which dealt with engineering problems. At the time I worked there (1977-83) these problems were of two kinds: machine shops and other small and large companies came to us with blueprints from which we were to produce "part-programs" for their numerically controlled machine tools such as mills, drills, punch presses, flame cutters, and lathes. We also developed software to assisted with producing and checking those part programs. Some software was for general use, and we had customers who used our programs on our time-share systems. Some was *ad hoc*: special programs written solely for our own internal use, often to assist with just a single kind of problem. This was typically because we rarely had the time to generalize these tools to the style and reliability desirable and necessary for use by customers. We "cobbled together" whatever was necessary to accomplish the task in hand, and while we often tried to make these *ad hoc* tools as general as possible, all too often that did not occur, because by the time we were almost done with one project, we had two or three new ones to work on. It was interesting; one never knew what new puzzle might walk in the door – see the first volume of my Case Studies for some examples.

One of these *ad hoc* tools was rather general, as it wasn't aimed at any particular "problem" as such, nor even any particular sort of machine tool. It was developed when we received a group of rather odd-looking prints, with large and relatively regular repeating rectangles of holes which were to be drilled into a chunk of metal, all of which were to be drilled with the same bit. I have none of the original problems to show you – I don't recall who it was for, or even what they were supposed to be – but here is a contrived example which will give you a hint of what they were like:

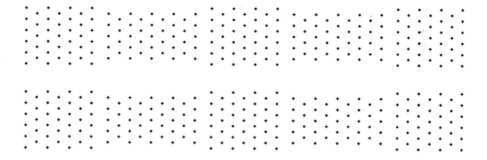

This sample is a good deal simpler and smaller than any of the real ones, which I think had thousands of points. The above diagram does not show any of the dimensions; of course the actual blueprints had all of those. As you may know, blueprints (like music, recipes, and programming) have tricks to simplify repetitive tasks, and they certainly did not draw *all* of the holes; they simply set down the repeat counts and spacings.

For our demonstration, we may assume that the rows and columns are regularly spaced at 20, with the alternate columns offset in Y by 10. The spacing between the rectangular groups is 30 in X and 50 in Y. Thus, letting the point in the upper right be 0,0, the corresponding point in the second rectangular group in the upper row is at 150,–10, while the corresponding point in the leftmost group of the lower row is at 0,–150.

Now, the NC drill which our customer was going to use was relatively simple: it had no sophisticated "grid" or "repeat" command, but was controlled simply by a series of X and Y statements which showed *how far* (the *incremental* distance) the tool was to advance from its present position. After it moved a hole would be drilled at that location. If either coordinate was omitted, that one stayed the same from line to line. The instructions were therefore of these forms:

X*xshift*Y*yshift**   representing a diagonal move by (*xshift,yshift*)
X*xshift**   representing a horizontal move by (*xshift*,0)
Y*yshift**   representing a vertical move by (0,*yshift*)

So for something like this, the part-program was very simple, just a series of repeated vertical moves, with intervening instructions to shift between columns or between groups. All of the blueprints were similar in that sense, but the repetitions and dimensions were quite different, and so Charlie Blouch, the head of NC, and I talked about how we might build something that wasn't really an *engineering* sort of tool, but that worked at the *string* level: that is, something which took *arbitrary strings* (as we have been discussing in this book, a series of characters) and arranged them in repetitive patterns in an output file. We could use integers and grouping tricks (like parentheses) to mark repeats as necessary. For eaxmple, if "A" is our vertical move (go down by 20) repeated five times, and B the move to advance to the right by one column (go right 20 and up 10), we could do the first column by something like this:
A="Y–20*"
B="X+20Y+10*"
CL=5A,B

Then we need to go back up four times, and move to the top of the next column:
C="Y+20*"
D="X+20Y+10*"
CR=4C,D

(Yes, I am aware that here D is the same as B, but maybe in the real problems that was not the case.) So we could represent the first pair of columns with
PAIR=CL,CR
and the first entire rectangle with:
RECT=3PAIR,5A

This sort of program was far easier to develop than any sort of geometric arrangement which declared points by grids, as the grids are not regular, and so there would be backtracking – that is, the actual drilling task would take a good deal longer to do because the tool would have to move back to do the other set of grids... and if we tried that, we would run into an issue of *optimization*.[79]

Often the hardest task in programming is to pick a suitable name. But I got this idea of linking a name to a fixed string from the "micros" in the COMPASS

---

[79] This is a very fascinating problem which we treat at length in *Sometimes*, the fourth volume of this series.

assembler for the CDC 6400 which I had learned while at college.[80] And so we called this tool the MICRO.

By careful study of the repeated elements of the blueprint, and computing the incremental distances, it was very easy to devise an input to the program. Here is the one for the above design:

```
a="y-20*"
b="x+20y+10*"
c="y+20*"
d="x+20y+10*"
e=5a,b,4c,d
f="x+30y+90*"
g=3e,5a
h=4a,b,3c,d
i=4h,4a
j="x+30y+90*"
n=g,f,i,j
y="x+0*"
m="x-800y+250*"
z=y,2n,g,m,2n,g
```

The expansion of "z", the last of these "micros," results in the following series:

```
YAAAAABCCCDAAAAABCCCDAAAAABCCCDAAAAAFAAAABCCCDAAAABCCCDAAAABCCCDAA
AABCCCDAAAAJAAAAABCCCDAAAAABCCCDAAAAABCCCDAAAAAFAAAABCCCDAAAABCCCD
AAAABCCCDAAAABCCCDAAAAJAAAAABCCCDAAAAABCCCDAAAAABCCCDAAAAMAAAAABC
CCCDAAAAABCCCDAAAAABCCCDAAAAAFAAAABCCCDAAAABCCCDAAAABCCCDAAAABCCCDA
AAAJAAAAABCCCDAAAAABCCCDAAAAABCCCDAAAAAFAAAABCCCDAAAABCCCDAAAABCCC
DAAAABCCCDAAAAJAAAAABCCCDAAAAABCCCDAAAAABCCCDAAAAA
```

These expanded to 398 XY lines which we omit, but the above diagram was generated by means of this sequence.[81] With this tool, it was easy to write instructions to generate the part-programs from our customer's blueprints, and we soon had them completed. We checked the results by use of our "plot generator" which produced diagrams (like the above) from the final part-program. These were drawn to scale, and enabled the customer to verify the correctness of our work.

---

[80] A "macro" had parameters, and so could be expanded in various ways; a "micro" was merely a shorthand for another string, which was always expanded the same way.
[81] I did not use the original program, which has long since vanished into oblivion, but it was easy enough to reconstruct enough functionality to accomplish the task. I should probably add that certain initialization and termination instructions specific to the customer's machine tool were necessary, so we could have written something like this:
```
        startup="SpecialStartUpCodes*"
        final="SpecialFinalCodes*"
        partprogram=startup,part,final
```
then had the MICRO tool expand "partprogram" into an output file.

3. CASE STUDY: UNIQUE STRINGS

Often we will wish to investigate an algorithm with a "test collection" of strings, and it is handy to have such things available. In the general case, of course, when we have a given alphabet A, the number of possible strings of length k is given by $(card(A))^k$. Aspects and limits of biology, biochemistry, and chemistry may impose their own requirements on this collection, but from a purely string-theoretic perspective, there is little reason to distinguish between any one character and another, so it is reasonable to provide a test collection of strings which are unique *up to substitution* of one character for another.

Thus, for A_{DNA} = {a, c, g, t} and length k=3, we have 4^3 = 64 *distinct* strings, which can be reduced to the following five *unique* strings:

unique	representing
aaa	aaa, ccc, ggg, ttt
aac	aac, cca, aag, gga, aat, tta, ccg, ggc, cct, ttc, ggt, ttg
aca	aca, cac, aga, gag, ata, tat, cgc, gcg, ctc, tct, gtg, tgt
acc	acc, caa, agg, gaa, att, taa, cgg, gcc, ctt, tcc, gtt, tgg
acg	acg, act, agc, agt, atc, atg, cag, cat, cga, cgt, cta, ctg, gac, gat, gca, gct, gta, gtc, tac, tag, tca, tcg, tga, tgc

The algorithm to produce such strings is a simple application of recursion. We are given the Alphabet with AlphaSize characters, and we specify the length *desired* of the unique strings desired. Then, having set buffer[1] to the first character of the alphabet, call GenerateUniqueStrings(1,1,desired).

```
Procedure GenerateUniqueStrings
arguments
   in integer depth
   in integer distinctcharsinprefix
   in integer desired
local
   integer j
global
   character Alphabet[]
   integer AlphaSize
   string buffer
begin
   if depth > desired then
      ;; buffer contains the next unique string
      ;; output or save it as needed
   else
      For j ← 1 to distinctcharsinprefix do
            buffer[depth+1] ← Alphabet[j]
            MakeUniqueWords(depth+1,distinctcharsinprefix,desired)
      Endfor ;; j
      if distinctcharsinprefix < AlphaSize then
            buffer[depth+1] ← Alphabet[distinctcharsinprefix+1]
            MakeUniqueWords(depth+1,distinctcharsinprefix+1,desired)
      Endif
Endproc
```

The following table gives the first few values of the number of *distinct* strings and *unique* strings over A_{DNA} for varying lengths k:

k	distinct T(k)	a N(k,1)	ac N(k,2)	acg N(k,3)	acgt N(k,4)	unique U(k)
1	4	1	0	0	0	1
2	16	1	1	0	0	2
3	64	1	3	1	0	5
4	256	1	7	6	1	15
5	1024	1	15	25	10	51
6	4096	1	31	90	65	187
7	16384	1	63	301	350	715
8	65536	1	127	966	1701	2795
9	262144	1	255	3025	7770	11051
10	1048576	1	511	9330	34105	43947
11	4194304	1	1023	28501	145750	175275
12	16777216	1	2047	86526	611501	700075

The total number of strings of length k over an alphabet of size 4 is
$$T(k) = 4^k$$
The number of unique strings is given by
$$U(k) = N(k,1) + N(k,2) + N(k,3) + N(k,4)$$
where $N(k, d)$ is the number of strings of length k having d distinct letters:
$$N(1,1) = 1$$
for $d>k$,
$$N(k, d) = 0$$
for $k>1$,
$$N(k,1) = 1$$
$$N(k,2) = 1 + 2 \cdot N(k-1,2)$$
$$N(k,3) = N(k-1,2) + 3 \cdot N(k-1,3)$$
$$N(k,4) = N(k-1,3) + 4 \cdot N(k-1,4)$$

These recurrence formulas can be reduced to closed forms:[82]
$$N(k,1) = 1$$
$$N(k,2) = 2^{k-1} - 1$$
$$N(k,3) = (3^{k-1}-1)/2 - 2^{k-1} + 1$$
$$N(k,4) = (4^{k-1} - 3 \cdot 3^{k-1} + 3 \cdot 2^{k-1} - 1)/6$$
hence
$$U(k) = (4^{k-1} + 3 \cdot 2^{k-1} + 2)/6$$

---

[82] See the Generating Function technique for solving recurrences, e.g. Roberts, *Applied Combinatorics*, 218-221.

List of unique strings over A_{DNA} for $k \leq 5$

k=2
1 aa
2 ac

k=3
1 aaa
2 aac
3 aca
4 acc
5 acg

k=4
1 aaaa
2 aaac
3 aaca
4 aacc
5 aacg
6 acaa
7 acac
8 acag
9 acca
10 accc
11 accg
12 acga
13 acgc
14 acgg
15 acgt

k=5
1 aaaaa
2 aaaac
3 aaaca
4 aaacc
5 aaacg
6 aacaa
7 aacac
8 aacag
9 aacca
10 aaccc
11 aaccg
12 aacga
13 aacgc
14 aacgg
15 aacgt
16 acaaa
17 acaac
18 acaag
19 acaca
20 acacc
21 acacg
22 acaga
23 acagc
24 acagg
25 acagt
26 accaa
27 accac
28 accag
29 accca
30 acccc
31 acccg
32 accga
33 accgc
34 accgg
35 accgt
36 acgaa
37 acgac
38 acgag
39 acgat
40 acgca
41 acgcc
42 acgcg
43 acgct
44 acgga
45 acggc
46 acggg
47 acggt
48 acgta
49 acgtc
50 acgtg
51 acgtt

* * *

What happens for alphabets of other sizes?

The total number of strings of length k over an alphabet of size n is
$$T_n(k) = n^k$$
The number of unique strings is given by
$$U_n(k) = \sum_{i=1}^{n} N_n(k,i)$$
where $N_n(k, d)$ is the number of strings over an alphabet of n characters with length k having d distinct letters; the recurrence formula is
$$N_n(1,1) = 1$$
for $d > k$,
$$N_n(k, d) = 0$$
for $k > 1$,
$$N_n(k, d) = N_n(k-1, d-1) + d \cdot N(k-1, d)$$
(Note that this recurrence produces the equations given above for $n=4$.)

The closed form for $N_n(k, d)$ is:
$$N_n(k, d) = \frac{\sum_{j=1}^{d} -1^{d-j} \cdot j^{k-1} \cdot \binom{d-1}{j-1}}{(d-1)!} = \sum_{j=1}^{d} -1^{d-j} \cdot \frac{j^{k-1}}{(d-j)!(j-1)!}$$

For example, the counts of unique strings for the alphabet {a, b, c, d, e}:

k	distinct $T_5(k)$	a $N_5(k,1)$	ab $N_5(k,2)$	abc $N_5(k,3)$	abcd $N_5(k,4)$	abcde $N_5(k,5)$	unique $U_5(k)$
1	5	1	0	0	0	0	1
2	25	1	1	0	0	0	2
3	125	1	3	1	0	0	5
4	625	1	7	6	1	0	15
5	3125	1	15	25	10	1	52
6	15625	1	31	90	65	15	202
7	78125	1	63	301	350	140	855
8	390625	1	127	966	1701	1050	3845
9	1953125	1	255	3025	7770	6951	18002
10	9765625	1	511	9330	34105	42525	86472
11	48828125	1	1023	28501	145750	246730	422005
12	244140625	1	2047	86526	611501	1379400	2079475

Note that the counts in the first four columns (a, ab, abc, abcd) are identical to those given in the previous table for the alphabet of size four.

4. CASE STUDY: THE OMNIWORD

In the previous case study we considered the collections of unique strings. This suggests an associated question: Given an alphabet A of n characters, find a string over A which contains *all* substrings of a given length. We define an *omniword* $\Omega(n,k)$ for an alphabet of n characters to be a string which contains every possible substring of length k over that alphabet.

Clearly, there are n^k distinct substrings over A of length k, so there always exists a string of length $k \cdot n^k$ formed by concatenating every such substring.

For example, if A = {a, b}, for $k = 2$, the substrings are aa, ab, ba, bb. The string "aaabbabb" contains all of them. Hence $len(\Omega(n,k)) \leq k \cdot n^k$.

However, in this example there are clearly repeated instances of some substrings, so there could be shorter examples. In fact, the string "aabba" also contains all four substrings. Due to the pigeonhole principle, the omniword cannot contain fewer than $n^k + k - 1$ characters, since otherwise there would not be n^k distinct substrings. Hence we must have:

$$n^k + k - 1 \leq len(\Omega(n,k)) \leq k \cdot n^k.$$

If we are given an omniword $\omega = \Omega(n,k)$ for some alphabet, it is clear that its reverse, $\omega' = reverse(\omega)$, is also an omniword. In our example, the reverse of "aabba" is "abbaa" which clearly contains all four substrings of length two.

Conjecture: Given an alphabet A of n symbols and an integer k greater than one, the omniword $\Omega(n,k)$ exists and has length $n^k + k - 1$. That is, there exists a string over A of length $n^k + k - 1$ which contains all strings in A* of length k as substrings of $\Omega(n,k)$.[83]

It is straightforward to arrange a program[84] to compute such strings. In fact, experimentation for a few small integers shows that there are multiple omniwords to be found, and they indeed have the minimum length, $n^k + k - 1$. Upon investigation, we found that some solutions are related to others, either by a circular derangement, or by permutation (substitution) of the characters of the alphabet. Hence, we include the count of *unique* omniwords as well:

n	k	omniwords	unique	example solution
2	2	1	1	aabba
2	3	2	1	aaababbbaa
2	4	16	8	aaaabaabbababbbbaaa
2	5	2048	1024	aaaaabaaabbaababaabbbababbabbbbbaaaa
3	2	12	6	aabacbbcca
3	3	186624	93312	aaabaacabbabcacbaccbbbcbcccaa
4	2	82944	1728	aabacadbbcbdccdda

---

[83] I term this a *conjecture* as I have not yet been able to establish this formally. So far my experimental testing suggests that it is true.
[84] It proceeds in the usual recursive (depth-first) search; as yet I have not been able to find a direct way of computing an omniword.

Having observed this replication of solutions by reversal or circular derangement, a circular nature seems to be hinted at. For example, when $n=2$ and $k=3$, one may arrange the omniword $\Omega(2,3)$ = "aaababbbaa" around a circle:

The annulus for omniword $\Omega(2,3)$ = "aaababbbaa"

The annulus is an object like a string but has neither beginning nor end, and we represent it by this symbol:
[aaababbbaa]

This notation is for convenience of discussion, and it must be emphasized that the object represented is *not* a string; it is a circular arrangement of characters. Further study of the annulus will be presented in a future edition.

Here is another example:

The annulus for omniword $\Omega(2,4)$ = "aaaabaabbabababbbaaa"

Such a circle of characters corresponding to an omniword has n^k characters, and we note that each character of A will appear exactly n^{k-1} times in it. Clearly, the circular arrangement can always be altered into a corresponding string by cutting it and adding enough characters to fill out the final substring at the tail. The diagram reveals the redundancies arising from (1) traversing the circle either clockwise or counter-clockwise, or (2) cutting at any point and adding the requisite characters to complete the final substring.

This circular quality suggests that the question can be transformed into a number-theoretic question based upon the modulus, wherein strings are mapped to integers:

Let $n = card(A)$, and let the characters of A be mapped to the integers 0, 1, ... $n-1$:
$map(a_i) = i-1$
for each a_i in A.

Then we map the strings α over A to integers between 0 and $n^{len(\alpha)}-1$:

$$map(\alpha) = \sum_{j=1}^{|\alpha|} map(\alpha_j) n^{|\alpha|-j-1}$$

For some given k with $N=n^k$, we wish to find the string ω of length $N+k-1$ which yields a sequence $[p_i]$ of the integers between 0 and $N-1$, which are the mappings of each of its substrings of length k:

$p_i = map(\omega[i \text{ for } k])$ for $1 \leq i \leq N$

This sequence of p_i is a permutation of the integers between 0 and $N-1$ subject to:
$p_i = (n \cdot p_{i-1} + j_{i-1}) \mod N$ with $0 \leq j_{i-1} < n$ and $1 < i \leq N$
and
$p_1 = (n \cdot p_N + j_N) \mod N$ with $0 \leq j_N < n$

The value of each j_i must be chosen such that no two values are the same:
$p_g \neq p_h$ for $1 \leq g \leq N$ and $1 \leq h \leq N$

This computation has the effect of appending the j-th character of the alphabet to the substring represented by the previous substring and removing the first character of the result.

Thus, in our example with $n=2$, $k=2$, with $map(a)=0$ and $map(b)=1$, we have:
map(aa) = 0
map(ab) = 1
map(ba) = 2
map(bb) = 3
so for the string "aabba" we have the permutation
0, 1, 3, 2.

Taking the above example with $n=2$ and $k=3$ for "aaababbbaa":

a
b   a
b   a
b   b
a

By considering each triple going clockwise:
aaa, aab, aba, bab, abb, bbb, bba, baa
and letting these represent numbers in base-two (mapping a to 0, b to 1) we get the sequence
0, 1, 2, 5, 3, 7, 6, 4
corresponding to the following diagram:

```
        0
    4       1
  6           2
    7       5
        3
```

Another example, with *n*=3 and *k*=2, letting *map*(a)=0, *map*(b)=1 and *map*(c)=2:
    map(aa) = 0
    map(ab) = 1
    map(ac) = 2
    map(ba) = 3
    map(bb) = 4
    map(bc) = 5
    map(ca) = 6
    map(cb) = 7
    map(cc) = 8
Then the string "aabacbbcca" gives the permutation:
    0, 1, 3, 2, 7, 4, 5, 8, 6
as seen in the following diagrams:

```
         a                          0
      c     a                    6     1
    c         b                8         3
      b     a                    5     2
         b  c                       4  7
```

* * *

A Conclusion: When the Word is a Character

> ...it is extraordinary how very little there is in the recorded words of Christ that ties him at all to his own time. I do not mean the details of a period, which even a man of the period knows to be passing. I mean the fundamentals which even the wisest man often vaguely assumes to be eternal. For instance, Aristotle was perhaps the wisest and most wide-minded man who ever lived. He founded himself entirely upon fundamentals, which have been generally found to remain rational and solid through all social and historical changes. Still, he lived in a world in which it was thought as natural to have slaves as to have children. And therefore he did permit himself a serious recognition of a difference between slaves and free men. Christ as much as Aristotle lived in a world that took slavery for granted. He did not particularly denounce slavery. He started a movement that could exist in a world with slavery. But he started a movement that could exist in a world without slavery. He never used a phrase that made his philosophy depend even upon the very existence of the social order in which he lived. He spoke as one conscious that everything was ephemeral, including the things that Aristotle thought eternal. By that time the Roman Empire had come to be merely the *orbis terrarum*, another name for the world. But he never made his morality dependent on the existence of the Roman Empire or even on the existence of the world.
>
> GKC *The Everlasting Man* CW2:326-7

As a concluding observation, let us see what happens when the *word* itself is a character: that is, when we apply a tool like the CIF to English text in order to find repeated phrases of *words*, rather than merely repeated substrings.

This issue arose in my work on the electronic texts of G. K. Chesterton. His friend Hilaire Belloc wrote a book about GKC in which he writes:

> Whenever Chesterton begins a sentence with, "It is as though," (in exploding a false bit of reasoning,) you may expect a stroke of parallelism as vivid as a lightning flash.[85]

However, I was curious about this, and after some research with my complete electronic collection of GKC's books, I found that "it is as though" appears only *three* times, while "it is as if" appears over 250 times.

This led me to wonder what might be the longest repeated sequence of words in GKC's texts.

So, after having re-implemented in "C" the experimental program for finding signature strings discussed earlier, I revised it so that the atomic elements analyzed were English *words* (and punctuation) rather than the ASCII characters; I omitted the blanks between words, paragraphing and larger typographical elements.

This revision is, of course, straightforward, and took very little effort. Then I ran it against the electronic text for a particular book. The program worked well, and it gave an interesting result. The longest repeated word sequence in GKC's *The Everlasting Man* is this significant passage:

"Heaven and earth shall pass away; but my words shall not pass away."[86]

* * *

---

[85] Belloc, *On the Place of Gilbert Chesterton in English Letters*, 37
[86] GKC *The Everlasting Man* CW2:327 and 392, and citing Luke 21:33.

APPENDIX 1: THE CODES OF MOLECULAR BIOLOGY

The Nucleotide Wildcards

The codes for the standard nucleotide wildcards have a mnemonic basis in the underlying organic chemistry. The following explanation is paraphrased from that given in the standard.[87]

We give the wildcards for A_{DNA}, which are based on the DNA alphabet
$$A_{DNA} = \{a, c, g, t\}$$
The RNA alphabet simply replaces the "t" (for thymine) with "u" (for uracil).

Eigencharacters:
The nucleotide bases are:
- **A**   from a for adenine
- **C**   from c for cytosine
- **G**   from g for guanine
- **T**   from t for thymine (in DNA)
- **U**   from u for uracil (in RNA)

Degree 2 characters:
- **R**=(a,g)   adenine and guanine are purines
- **Y**=(c,t/u)   cytosine and thymine/uracil are pyrimidines
- **M**=(a,c)   adenine and cytosine have a**m**ino groups (NH_2)
- **K**=(g,t/u)   guanine and thymine/uracil have **k**eto groups (C=O)
- **S**=(c,g)   cytosine-guanine has 3 hydrogen bonds "**s**trong"
- **W**=(a,t/u)   adenine-thymine/uracil has 2 hydrogen bonds "**w**eak"

Degree 3 characters:
- **B**=(c,g,t)   not adenine (b is the letter after a)
- **D**=(a,g,t)   not cytosine (d is the letter after c)
- **H**=(a,c,t)   not guanine (h is the letter after g)
- **V**=(a,c,g)   not thymine/uracil (v is the letter after t/u)

Omni-match:
- **N**=(a,c,g,t) (the n from a**N**y)

(This symbol is standardized to N, though it appears as X in some papers.)

---

[87] Nomenclature Committee of the International Union of Biochemistry. Nomenclature for incompletely specified bases in nucleic acid sequences. *Eur. J. Biochem.* 150 (1985) 1-5.

The Genetic Code

```
AAA Lysine         CAA Glutamine      GAA Glutamic acid   TAA trm (ochre)
AAC Asparagine     CAC Histidine      GAC Aspartic acid   TAC Tyrosine
AAG Lysine         CAG Glutamine      GAG Glutamic acid   TAG trm (amber)
AAT Asparagine     CAT Histidine      GAT Aspartic acid   TAT Tyrosine
ACA Threonine      CCA Proline        GCA Alanine         TCA Serine
ACC Threonine      CCC Proline        GCC Alanine         TCC Serine
ACG Threonine      CCG Proline        GCG Alanine         TCG Serine
ACT Threonine      CCT Proline        GCT Alanine         TCT Serine
AGA Arginine       CGA Arginine       GGA Glycine         TGA trm (opal)
AGC Serine         CGC Arginine       GGC Glycine         TGC Cysteine
AGG Arginine       CGG Arginine       GGG Glycine         TGG Tryptophan
AGT Serine         CGT Arginine       GGT Glycine         TGT Cysteine
ATA Isoleucine     CTA Leucine        GTA Valine          TTA Leucine
ATC Isoleucine     CTC Leucine        GTC Valine          TTC Phenylalanine
ATG Methionine     CTG Leucine        GTG Valine          TTG Leucine
ATT Isoleucine     CTT Leucine        GTT Valine          TTT Phenylalanine
```

The underlying two-base table (showing effect of wobble base)

	A	C	G	T
A	Lys/Asn	Gln/His	Glu/Asp	trm/Tyr
C	Thr	Pro	Ala	Ser
G	Arg/Ser	Arg	Gly	trm/Cys/Trp
T	Ile/Met	Leu	Val	Leu/Phe

The amino acids

codes		name	#	codons (in the wildcard alphabet)
A	Ala	Alanine	4	GCN
R	Arg	Arginine	6	CGN, AGR
N	Asn	Asparagine	2	AAY
D	Asp	Aspartic acid	2	GAY
C	Cys	Cysteine	2	TGY
E	Glu	Glutamic acid	2	GAR
Q	Gln	Glutamine	2	CAR
G	Gly	Glycine	4	GGN
H	His	Histidine	2	CAY
I	Ile	Isoleucine	3	ATH
L	Leu	Leucine	4	CTN
K	Lys	Lysine	2	AAR
M	Met	Methionine	1	ATG
F	Phe	Phenylalanine	2	TTY
P	Pro	Proline	4	CCN
S	Ser	Serine	6	TCN, AGY
T	Thr	Threonine	4	ACN
W	Trp	Tryptophan	1	TGG
Y	Tyr	Tyrosine	2	TAY
V	Val	Valine	4	GTN
	trm	terminator	3	TAR, TGA

Unused letters in amino acid codes: B J O U X Z

Note that there are a few minor exceptions to this code, occurring in mitochondria and certain protozoa. See (e.g.) Rawn, *Biochemistry*, 826 for further details.

APPENDIX 2: EIGHT BITS OR ONE BYTE

The 256 possible eight-bit values, written in binary, octal, hexadecimal, and decimal:

```
binary oct hx dec   binary  oct hx dec   binary   oct hx dec   binary   oct hx dec

     0 000 00   0   1000000 100 40  64   10000000 200 80 128   11000000 300 c0 192
     1 001 01   1   1000001 101 41  65   10000001 201 81 129   11000001 301 c1 193
    10 002 02   2   1000010 102 42  66   10000010 202 82 130   11000010 302 c2 194
    11 003 03   3   1000011 103 43  67   10000011 203 83 131   11000011 303 c3 195
   100 004 04   4   1000100 104 44  68   10000100 204 84 132   11000100 304 c4 196
   101 005 05   5   1000101 105 45  69   10000101 205 85 133   11000101 305 c5 197
   110 006 06   6   1000110 106 46  70   10000110 206 86 134   11000110 306 c6 198
   111 007 07   7   1000111 107 47  71   10000111 207 87 135   11000111 307 c7 199
  1000 010 08   8   1001000 110 48  72   10001000 210 88 136   11001000 310 c8 200
  1001 011 09   9   1001001 111 49  73   10001001 211 89 137   11001001 311 c9 201
  1010 012 0a  10   1001010 112 4a  74   10001010 212 8a 138   11001010 312 ca 202
  1011 013 0b  11   1001011 113 4b  75   10001011 213 8b 139   11001011 313 cb 203
  1100 014 0c  12   1001100 114 4c  76   10001100 214 8c 140   11001100 314 cc 204
  1101 015 0d  13   1001101 115 4d  77   10001101 215 8d 141   11001101 315 cd 205
  1110 016 0e  14   1001110 116 4e  78   10001110 216 8e 142   11001110 316 ce 206
  1111 017 0f  15   1001111 117 4f  79   10001111 217 8f 143   11001111 317 cf 207
 10000 020 10  16   1010000 120 50  80   10010000 220 90 144   11010000 320 d0 208
 10001 021 11  17   1010001 121 51  81   10010001 221 91 145   11010001 321 d1 209
 10010 022 12  18   1010010 122 52  82   10010010 222 92 146   11010010 322 d2 210
 10011 023 13  19   1010011 123 53  83   10010011 223 93 147   11010011 323 d3 211
 10100 024 14  20   1010100 124 54  84   10010100 224 94 148   11010100 324 d4 212
 10101 025 15  21   1010101 125 55  85   10010101 225 95 149   11010101 325 d5 213
 10110 026 16  22   1010110 126 56  86   10010110 226 96 150   11010110 326 d6 214
 10111 027 17  23   1010111 127 57  87   10010111 227 97 151   11010111 327 d7 215
 11000 030 18  24   1011000 130 58  88   10011000 230 98 152   11011000 330 d8 216
 11001 031 19  25   1011001 131 59  89   10011001 231 99 153   11011001 331 d9 217
 11010 032 1a  26   1011010 132 5a  90   10011010 232 9a 154   11011010 332 da 218
 11011 033 1b  27   1011011 133 5b  91   10011011 233 9b 155   11011011 333 db 219
 11100 034 1c  28   1011100 134 5c  92   10011100 234 9c 156   11011100 334 dc 220
 11101 035 1d  29   1011101 135 5d  93   10011101 235 9d 157   11011101 335 dd 221
 11110 036 1e  30   1011110 136 5e  94   10011110 236 9e 158   11011110 336 de 222
 11111 037 1f  31   1011111 137 5f  95   10011111 237 9f 159   11011111 337 df 223
100000 040 20  32   1100000 140 60  96   10100000 240 a0 160   11100000 340 e0 224
100001 041 21  33   1100001 141 61  97   10100001 241 a1 161   11100001 341 e1 225
100010 042 22  34   1100010 142 62  98   10100010 242 a2 162   11100010 342 e2 226
100011 043 23  35   1100011 143 63  99   10100011 243 a3 163   11100011 343 e3 227
100100 044 24  36   1100100 144 64 100   10100100 244 a4 164   11100100 344 e4 228
100101 045 25  37   1100101 145 65 101   10100101 245 a5 165   11100101 345 e5 229
100110 046 26  38   1100110 146 66 102   10100110 246 a6 166   11100110 346 e6 230
100111 047 27  39   1100111 147 67 103   10100111 247 a7 167   11100111 347 e7 231
101000 050 28  40   1101000 150 68 104   10101000 250 a8 168   11101000 350 e8 232
101001 051 29  41   1101001 151 69 105   10101001 251 a9 169   11101001 351 e9 233
101010 052 2a  42   1101010 152 6a 106   10101010 252 aa 170   11101010 352 ea 234
101011 053 2b  43   1101011 153 6b 107   10101011 253 ab 171   11101011 353 eb 235
101100 054 2c  44   1101100 154 6c 108   10101100 254 ac 172   11101100 354 ec 236
101101 055 2d  45   1101101 155 6d 109   10101101 255 ad 173   11101101 355 ed 237
101110 056 2e  46   1101110 156 6e 110   10101110 256 ae 174   11101110 356 ee 238
101111 057 2f  47   1101111 157 6f 111   10101111 257 af 175   11101111 357 ef 239
110000 060 30  48   1110000 160 70 112   10110000 260 b0 176   11110000 360 f0 240
110001 061 31  49   1110001 161 71 113   10110001 261 b1 177   11110001 361 f1 241
110010 062 32  50   1110010 162 72 114   10110010 262 b2 178   11110010 362 f2 242
110011 063 33  51   1110011 163 73 115   10110011 263 b3 179   11110011 363 f3 243
110100 064 34  52   1110100 164 74 116   10110100 264 b4 180   11110100 364 f4 244
110101 065 35  53   1110101 165 75 117   10110101 265 b5 181   11110101 365 f5 245
110110 066 36  54   1110110 166 76 118   10110110 266 b6 182   11110110 366 f6 246
110111 067 37  55   1110111 167 77 119   10110111 267 b7 183   11110111 367 f7 247
111000 070 38  56   1111000 170 78 120   10111000 270 b8 184   11111000 370 f8 248
111001 071 39  57   1111001 171 79 121   10111001 271 b9 185   11111001 371 f9 249
111010 072 3a  58   1111010 172 7a 122   10111010 272 ba 186   11111010 372 fa 250
111011 073 3b  59   1111011 173 7b 123   10111011 273 bb 187   11111011 373 fb 251
111100 074 3c  60   1111100 174 7c 124   10111100 274 bc 188   11111100 374 fc 252
111101 075 3d  61   1111101 175 7d 125   10111101 275 bd 189   11111101 375 fd 253
111110 076 3e  62   1111110 176 7e 126   10111110 276 be 190   11111110 376 fe 254
111111 077 3f  63   1111111 177 7f 127   10111111 277 bf 191   11111111 377 ff 255
```

The ASCII Character Set

(ASCII = American Standard Code for Information Interchange)

```
      0 1 2 3 4 5 6 7   8 9 a b c d e f
  2     ! " # $ % & '   ( ) * + , - . /
  3   0 1 2 3 4 5 6 7   8 9 : ; < = > ?
  4   @ A B C D E F G   H I J K L M N O
  5   P Q R S T U V W   X Y Z [ \ ] ^ _
  6   ` a b c d e f g   h i j k l m n o
  7   p q r s t u v w   x y z { | } ~ µ
```

An eight-bit byte provides 256 possible representations. However, ASCII was originally a *seven* bit code, with the eighth (topmost) bit used for parity: it was set so that every pattern contained an *even* number of bits which were one. Any character containing an *odd* number was deemed in error. It was not until later (maybe in the 1980s) that the above table became the usual representation, which relies on a "zero" parity. That is, the topmost bit is always zero, and no test for parity is performed. This presumably enabled another 128 characters, but of course there was no standard for what they are; now there are even larger encoding schemes, and the slow en-Babel-ing of the field creeps onwards, alas.

Also note that rows 0 and 1 were assigned to non-printing "control characters" such as 0001101, hex 0d is the "carriage return"; 0001010, hex 0a is "line feed"; the "ESCAPE" symbol is 0011011, hex 1b. (Note I have used the classic seven bits here.) The "carriage return" comes from the antecedent manual printing devices called "typewriters" as it "returned" the "carriage," effectively bringing the printhead back to the leftmost point in preparation for a new line of output; the "line-feed" ratcheted the carriage so that the paper advanced by one line. The "carriage return" is sometimes called the "Enter" key, though that may also be the "line-feed" depending; but it often has the effect of both, as some old-timers recall writing 13 and 10 (or 15, 12 in octal or 0xd, 0xa in hex).

APPENDIX 3: THE BLUMER DAWG/CIF ALGORITHM FOR SIGNATURES

The following pseudocode is revised from that given in my dissertation. It is based on the Blumer paper (except for Phase6 and Phase 7, which are the results of my own research.) and has also been checked against my functional implementation.

Inputs:
    Alphabet[] is the array of characters from which the source strings are formed.
    S[] is the array of strings for which signatures are desired.

Data Structures:

DAWGEdge
to	points to the destination DAWG node
primary	boolean flag specifying whether this edge is primary
s	string index for the label of this edge
e	end position for the label of this edge
k	length for the label of this edge

DAWGnode
index	a unique integer for debugging, description, etc.
visited	boolean indicating this node has been visited
InCIF	boolean indicating this node is in the CIF or DAWG (phase 4)
(label)	the label for this node is stored as three integers:
s	the string id which contains the label
e	the end position of the label
k	the length of the label

That is, the label is S[s][e **back** k], the substring of the input string s which ends at e and has k characters.

suffix	the suffix of this node.
ident	a list of ids of the strings which have this node's label as a suffix.
impptr	the implication pointer for this node.
implen	the implication length for this node.
freq	the frequency of this node (the number of times this label appears).
edge	the array of DAWGedges representing the edges out of this node.
topolink	a pointer to a node, forming the topological list of nodes in the CIF.
kernel	an integer representing the kernel length.
uniset	a set of card(S) elements, representing which elements of S are contained by the node or any of its descendents.

At creation of a node, all fields are set to zero or null, except for index, which is set to a unique integer for identification and debugging.

Blumer Phase 1
This phase builds the DAWG for a given set of strings, S. It produces the DAWG which is rooted at the pointer called source, also the array of pointers called final, which correspond to the array of strings. The main routine uses two ancillary routines, BlumerUpdate and BlumerSplit.

```
Procedure BlumerPhase1(S,source,final)
argument
    in string S[]
    out DAWGnode pointer source
    out DAWGnode pointer final[card(S)]
local
    integer i,j
    DAWGnode pointer active
begin

    source ← CreateNode(0,0,0)
    source→implen=-2

    for i ← 1 to card(S) do
        active ← source
        for j ← 1 to len(s[i]) do
            active ← BlumerUpdate(active,s[i][j for 1],i,j)
        endfor ;; character loop
        final[i] ← active
    endfor ;; string loop
endproc
```

```
procedure BlumerUpdate(activenode,c,s,e)
returns
    DAWGnode pointer
arguments
    in DAWGnode pointer activenode
    in character c
    in integer s
    in integer e
local
    DAWGnode pointer newnode
    DAWGnode pointer currentnode
    DAWGnode pointer suffixnode
    DAWGnode pointer child
begin

    newnode ← activenode→edge[c].ToNode
    If newnode ≠ NULL then
        ;; already have an edge from activenode on this character
        If activenode→edge[c].primary then
            Return newnode
        Else
            Return BlumerSplit(activenode,newnode,c)
        Endif
    Else
        ;; no edge from activenode on character c
        ;; create new node and edge
        newnode ← CreateNode(s,e,(activenode→k)+1)
        activenode→edge[c].ToNode ← newnode
        activenode→edge[c].primary ← TRUE

        currentnode ← activenode
        suffixnode ← NULL

        ;; walk the list of suffixes from the activenode
        ;; adding edges when needed

        While (currentnode ≠ source) and (suffixnode = NULL) do
            currentnode ← currentnode→suffix
            If currentnode→edge[c].ToNode ≠ NULL then
                If currentnode→edge[c].primary then
                    suffixnode ← currentnode→edge[c].ToNode
                Else
                    child ← currentnode→edge[c].ToNode
                    suffixnode ← BlumerSplit(currentnode,child,c)
                Endif
            Else
                ;; add edge on c
                currentnode→edge[c].ToNode ← newnode
                currentnode→edge[c].primary ← FALSE
            Endif
        Endwhile

        If suffixnode = NULL then
            suffixnode ← source
        Endif

        newnode→suffix ← suffixnode

        return newnode
    Endif
endproc
```

```
Procedure BlumerSplit(parent,child,c)
returns
    DAWGnode
arguments
    in DAWGnode pointer parent
    in DAWGnode pointer child
    in character c
local
    DAWGnode newnode
    DAWGnode currentnode
    character a
    boolean done
global
    character Alphabet[]
begin

    ;; create a new node where the split occurs
    newnode ← CreateNode(child→s, child→e, (parent→k)+1)
    parent→edge[c].ToNode ← newnode
    parent→edge[c].primary ← TRUE

    ;; duplicate the edges of the existing child into the new node
    For a in Alphabet do
        newnode→edge[a] ← child→edge[a]
        newnode→edge[a].primary ← FALSE
    Endfor ;; alphabet

    newnode→suffix ← child→suffix
    child→suffix ← newnode

    ;; walk the suffix list,
    ;; adjusting any pointers to the existing child
    ;; to now point to the new node

    currentnode ← parent
    done ← FALSE


    While currentnode ≠ source and not done do
        currentnode ← currentnode→suffix
        done ← TRUE
        For a in Alphabet do
            If currentnode→edge[a].ToNode = child and
                    not currentnode→edge[a].primary then
                currentnode→edge[a].ToNode ← newnode
                done ← FALSE
            Endif
        Endfor ;; alphabet
    Endwhile

    Return newnode

Endproc
```

Blumer phase 2

In phase 2, the ident lists are built. For each string in S, we start at its entry in the final array built in phase 1, and go up the chain of suffix pointers until we reach the source, adding this string id to the ident list of each node reached.

```
Procedure BlumerPhase2(source,final)
arguments
    in DAWGnode pointer source
    in DAWGnode pointer final[]
local
    integer i
    DAWGnode pointer p
begin
    For i ← 1 to card(S) do
        p ← final[i]
        Append i to p→ident
        While p→suffix ≠ NULL do
            p ← p→suffix
            Append i to p→ident
        Endwhile
    Endfor
Endproc
```

Blumer phase 3

In phase 3, we set the implication pointer and length for all nodes. We use a depth-first traversal of the DAWG, accomplished by an auxiliary recursive routine, Phase3Visit.

```
Procedure BlumerPhase3(source)
arguments
    in DAWGnode pointer source
begin
    ClearVisitedFlag(source)
    Phase3Visit(source)
Endproc

Procedure Phase3Visit(node)
arguments
    in DAWGnode pointer node
local
    character c
    integer num_edges
    DAWGnode pointer child
begin

    If node→visited then
        return
    endif
    node→visited ← TRUE

    num_edges ← 0

    For c in Alphabet do
        If node→edge[c].ToNode ≠ NULL then
            num_edges ← num_edges + 1
            child ← node→edge[c].ToNode
            Phase3Visit(child)
        Endif
    Endfor

    If num_edges = 1 and node→ident = NULL then
        node→imply ← child→imply
        node→implen ← (child→implen) + 1
    Else
        node→imply ← node
        node→implen ← 0
    Endif
Endproc
```

Blumer phase 4

Phase four also performs a depth-first traversal (by means of phase_4_visit), though not necessarily all nodes are visited. It produces the new edges of the CIF and their labels. This phase may also be used to condense the total memory in use by the CIF by eliminating unreached nodes, but we omit that portion of the algorithm.

```
Procedure BlumerPhase4(source)
arguments
    in DAWGnode pointer source
begin
    ClearVisitedFlag(source)
    Phase4Visit(source)
Endproc

Procedure Phase4Visit(node)
arguments
    in DAWGnode pointer node
local
    character c
    DAWGnode pointer child
begin
    If node→visited then
        return
    endif
    node→visited ← TRUE

    If not (node→InCIF) and (node→implen) = 0 then
        For c in Alphabet do
            If node→edge[c].ToNode ≠ NULL then
                child ← node→edge[c].ToNode
                ;; make an edge of the CIF
                node→edge[c].ToNode ← child→imply
                ;; make the label for this edge
                node→edge[c].s ← child→imply→s
                node→edge[c].e ← child→imply→e
                node→edge[c].k ← (child→implen) + 1
                Phase4Visit(node→edge[c].ToNode)
            Endif
        Endfor
        node→InCIF ← TRUE
    Endif

Endproc
```

Blumer Phase 5

This is the last of the Blumer phases. We do a depth-first traversal of the CIF, computing the frequency for each node.

```
Procedure BlumerPhase5(source)
arguments
    in DAWGnode pointer source
begin
    ClearVisitedFlag(source)
    Phase5Visit(source)
Endprocedure

Procedure Phase5Visit(node)
arguments
    in DAWGnode pointer node
locals
    integer k
    character c
begin
    If node→visited then
        return
    endif
    node→visited ← TRUE

    If node→InCIF and node→freq = 0 then
        k ← 0
        For c in Alphabet do
            If node→edge[c].ToNode ≠ NULL then
                Phase5Visit(node→edge[c].ToNode)
                k ← k + node→edge[c].ToNode→freq
            Endif
        Endfor
        node→freq ← k + card(node→ident)
    Endif
Endproc
```

Phase 6

This phase was added to those of the Blumer algorithm to prepare for the finding of signatures. It computes the topological order of the nodes of the CIF, and computes the kernel for their labels.

```
Procedure Phase6(source)
arguments
   in DAWGnode pointer source
locals
   DAWGnode pointer node
   character c
   int newkernel
   DAWGnode pointer TopoList
begin
   ClearVisitedFlag(source)

   ;; part 1: build the topological list
   TopoList ← NULL
   Phase6Visit(source,TopoList)

   ;; part 2: determine kernel in topo order

   TopoList→kernel ← 0

   node ← TopoList
   while node ≠ NULL
      For c in Alphabet do
         If node→edge[c].ToNode ≠ NULL then
            ;; fix kernel...
            newkernel ← node→kernel + node→edge[c].k;
            if newkernel < node→edge[c].ToNode→kernel then
               node→edge[c].ToNode→kernel ← newkernel
            endif
         endof
      node ← node→topoptr;
   endwhile

Endproc
```

```
Procedure Phase6Visit(node,TopoList)
arguments
    in DAWGnode pointer node
    DAWGnode pointer TopoList
locals
    integer outedgecount
    character c
    boolean ok
begin
    If node→visited then
        return
    endif
    node→visited ← TRUE

    node→kernel ← MAXINT ;; the maximum positive integer
    outedgecount ← 0
    ok ← TRUE

    For c in Alphabet do
        If node→edge[c].ToNode ≠ NULL then
            outedgecount ← outedgecount + 1
            If node→edge[c].ToNode→kernel = 0 then
                Phase6Visit(node→edge[c].ToNode)
            Endif
                If node→edge[c].ToNode→unique ≠ node→s then
                    ok ← FALSE
            Endif
        Endif
    Endfor

    ;; unique? check ident ptr

    if (node→ident = NULL) or
        (card(node→ident) = 1 and node→ident = node→s)
        if outedgecount = 0 or ok then
            node→unique ← node->s
        endif
    endif

    ;; append the node to front of topological list
    node→topoptr ← TopoList
    TopoList ← node

Endproc
```

Phase 7

This phase was added to those of the Blumer algorithm in order to determine signatures.

```
Procedure Phase7(source,TopoList)
arguments
   in DAWGnode pointer source
   out DAWGnode pointer TopoList
locals
   DAWGnode pointer node
begin
   ClearVisitedFlag(source)
   Phase7Visit(source)
endproc

Procedure Phase7Visit(node)
arguments
   in DAWGnode pointer node
locals
   integer outedgecount
   character c
   boolean ok
begin
   If node→visited then
      return
   Endif
   node→visited ← TRUE

   For c in Alphabet do
      If node→edge[c].ToNode ≠ NULL then
         If node→edge[c].ToNode→unique = 0
            Phase7Walk(node→edge[c].ToNode)
         else
            ;; this node has a unique limb
            if node→suffix ≠ NULL then
               ;;Find the matching edge from the suffix
               if node→suffix→edge[c].ToNode ≠ NULL then
                  if node→suffix→edge[c].ToNode ≠
                           node→edge[c].ToNode and
                     node→suffix→edge[c].ToNode→unique ≠
                           node→edge[c].ToNode→unique then

                        ;; here, we may report a signature
                        ;; for string S[node→edge[c].s]
                        ;; ending at node→edge[c].e
                        ;; and having length node→edge[c].k

                  endif
               endif
            endif
         endif
      endif
   endfor
endproc
```

125

BIBLIOGRAPHY

Note: All Bible quotes are from the Douay-Rheims version.

Aho, Alfred V. & Ullmann, Jeffrey D. *Principles of Compiler Design.* (Reading, MA: Addison-Wesley, 1977).

Aho, A. V., Hopcroft, J. E., and Ullman, J. D. *Data Structures and Algorithms* (Reading, MA: Addison-Wesley, 1983).

Autenreieth, Georg. *A Homeric Dictionary.* (Norman and London: University of Oklahoma Press, 1876, 1901).

Beeching, Jack. *The Galleys at Lepanto.* (New York: Charles Scribner's Sons, 1982).

Belloc, Hilaire. *On the Place of Gilbert Chesterton in English Letters.* (London: Sheed and Ward, 1940).

Blumer, A., Blumer, J., Haussler, D., McConnell, R., and Ehrenfeucht, A. Complete inverted files for efficient text retrieval. *JACM* 34, 3 (1987) 578-595.

Boethius. *The Consolation of Philosophy.* Translated by W. V. Cooper. (Chicago: Regnery Gateway, 1981).

Bombaugh, C.C.; Gardiner, Martin (editor and annotator) *Oddities and Curiosities of Words and Literature.* (New York: Dover Publications, Inc., 1961).

Cajori, Florian. *A History of Mathematical Notations.* (New York: Dover Publications, Inc., 1993).

Cardwell, Donald. *The Norton History of Technology.* (New York: W. W. Norton & Co., 1995).

Carroll, Lewis. *Alice in Wonderland and Other Favorites.* (New York: Washington Square Press, 1960). (The pen name of C. L. Dodgson; this volume includes *Alice's Adventures in Wonderland, Through the Looking-Glass,* and *The Hunting of the Snark.*)

Chesterton, G. K. His collected works (CW) are published by Ignatius Press in San Francisco.

—. *Alarms and Discursions.* (In CW 23)

—. *The Apostle and the Wild Ducks.*

—. *Autobiography.* (In CW16)

—. *Charles Dickens.* (In CW15)

—. *The Common Man.* (In CW 25)

—. *The Everlasting Man.* (In CW2)

—. *Heretics.* (In CW1)

—. *The Innocence of Father Brown.* (In CW12)

—. *Irish Impressions.* (In CW20)

—. *Lunacy and Letters.* (In CW 26)

—. *Illustrated London News* essays (In CW27-36)

—. *Orthodoxy.* (In CW1)

—. *The Poet and the Lunatics.* (In CW9)

—. *The Return of Don Quixote.* (In CW 8)

—. *Robert Browning.* (In CW 17)

—. *The Thing.* (In CW 3)

—. *St. Thomas Aquinas.* (In CW2)

—. *The Wisdom of Father Brown.* (In CW11/12)

—. *What's Wrong With the World.* (In CW4)

Cunningham, A. B. *Murder Before Midnight.* (New York: E. P. Dutton & Co., Inc., 1945).

Darnell, J., Lodish, H., and Baltimore, D. *Molecular Cell Biology.* (New York: Scientific American Books, 1990).

Euclid. *The Elements.* (New York: Dover Publications, Inc., 1956).

Frisher M. E., Floriani, P. J. and Nierzwicki-Baur, S. Differential sensitivity of 16S rRNA targeted oligonucleotide. *Canadian Journal of Microbiology* 42:1010, 1061-1071, NRC Research Press, 1996.

Gaskell, Philip. *A New Introduction to Bibliography.* (Oxford: At the Clarendon Press, 1972).

Gardiner, Sir Alan. *Egyptian Grammar.* (London: Oxford University Press, 1969).

Goodwin, William W. *A Greek Grammar.* (Boston: Ginn & Company, 1898).

Gray, Henry. *Gray's Anatomy.* (New York: Bounty Books, 1977).

Hellemans, Alexander, and Bunch, Bryan. *The Timetables of Science.* (New York: Simon and Schuster, 1988).

Jaki. S. L. *Praying the Psalms.* (Grand Rapids, MI: Wm. B. Eerdmans, 2000),

Juster, Norton. *The Phantom Tollbooth.* (New York: Random House, 1961).

Knuth. Donald A. *The Art of Computer Programming.* 3 vols. (Reading, MA: Addison-Wesley, 1973).

Lewin, B. *Genes*. (New York: Wiley, 1985).
Liddell, Henry George and Scott, Robert. *A Greek Lexicon*. (Oxford: at the Clarendon Press, 1953).
Mantinbrand, James H. *Dictionary of Latin Literature*. (New York: Philosophical Library, 1956).
Marietti, Peter. *The Lord's Prayer in 250 Languages*. (Rome: S. Consilii Propaganda Fidei, 1870).
Marrou, H. I. *A History of Education in Antiquity*. (New York: Sheed and Ward, 1956).
Maycock, A. L. *The Man Who Was Orthodox*. A Selection from the Uncollected Writings of G. K. Chesterton. (London: Dennis Dobson, 1963).
Newman, John Henry. *The Idea of a University*. (New York: Doubleday Image, 1959).
Nomenclature Committee of the International Union of Biochemistry. Nomenclature for incompletely specified bases in nucleic acid sequences. *Eur. J. Biochem.* 150 (1985) 1-5.
Rawn, J. David. *Biochemistry*. (Burlington, NC: Neil Patterson Publishers, 1989).
Roberts, Fred S. *Applied Combinatorics*. (Englewood Cliffs, NJ: Prentice-Hall, Inc., 1984).
Sedgewick, *Algorithms*. (Reading, MA: Addison-Wesley, 1983).
Stone, Harold S. *Discrete Mathematical Structures and Their Applications*. (Chicago: Science Research Associates, Inc., 1973).
Tarjan, Robert E. *Data Structures and Network Algorithms*. (Philadelphia: Society for Industrial and Applied Mathematics, 1983).
Taylor, Jerome. *The Didascalicon of Hugh of St. Victor*. (New York: Columbia University Press, 1961).
Traynham, James G. *Essays on the History of Organic Chemistry*. (Baton Rouge: Louisiana State University Press, 1987).
Ullman, B.L. and Henry, Norman E.. *Latin for Americans*. Second Book. (New York: The Macmillan Company, 1950).
Van Nostrand's Scientific Encyclopedia. (New York: D. Van Nostrand Co., 1938).
Ward, Maisie. *Gilbert Keith Chesterton*. (New York: Sheed and Ward, 1943).
—. *Return To Chesterton*. (New York: Sheed and Ward, 1952).

* * *

INDEX

Note: the symbol *p*†*n* indicates that the given term can be found in note *n* on page *p*.

αιτια 12†19
'απαξ λεγομενα 37
δισ λεγομενα 37
πυρσος 37
χειρ 12

5S 35†55
16S 29-31, 33, 35, 38-39, 81, 126
23S 35†55
45S 39

Abelian 21, 46
adenine 24, 39, 55, 111
aitch 9
aitia 12†19
alanine 40, 112
algorithm iii, vii, 31-32, 36, 48, 65, 67, 69-71, 74, 80-84, 86-88, 91-92, 94, 102, 115, 121, 123, 125-127
alphabet iii, vii, 4, 8-10, 12, 14-15, 17-18, 20, 22-24, 31, 36, 42-44, 46-52, 55-58, 60, 62, 65-66, 68-69, 74, 80-84, 86-89, 91-92, 102-106, 108, 111-112, 115, 118, 120-125
ambiguity 19†30, 38
ambiguous iii, 25, 35, 38
Ambrosian University v
amino acid 38-40, 112
amino groups 111
ammonium cyanate 24†36
ammonium sulfate 24†36
anastomosis vii†3
anatomy 4†6, 126
anticodon 40-41
antisymmetric 45-46
Aquinas, St. Thomas 17†27, 126
arepera 12†19
arginine 112
Aristotle 110
arsenic 6
asparagine 112
aspartic acid 112
associative 2-3, 23†33, 46
Autenreieth, Georg 126
automata 4, 17, 22-23, 81-82, 84, 88, 91-95
awakening iii, 96, 98
Azaz, King vi-vii

Bach, Johann Sebastian 31
bacteria 13, 25, 30, 32-35, 39, 63-64
base-inclusion 43-47, 49, 56-57, 62, 82
BASIC 15†24, 21, 28, 34, 96-98
Belloc, Hilaire 110, 126
biochemistry 12, 23, 33†52, 35†55, 40†64, 55, 102, 111-112, 127
biologist 29, 32
biology iii, vii, 12-14, 23-25, 27-29, 32, 35-37, 39-40, 42, 44, 55, 64-66, 102, 111, 126
bit vi-vii, 2, 6-7, 17, 21, 28, 33, 48, 55-56, 70, 82, 88-91, 99, 110, 114
Blouch, Charles H. 100
Blumer iii, 37, 74-76, 115, 119-123, 125-126
Boethius 126
Boole, George 45, 47, 51-52, 55, 60, 69†69, 82-83, 89, 115, 118, 124-125
Boolean algebra 47, 51-52, 55, 60

boustrophedon 11
Braun-Howland, Ellen ii, 28
Brown, Father ii, 5, 126
Browning, Robert 9†14, 126
brute-force iii, 67, 81-82
bucket-list 69-73
byte iii, 6-7, 9, 113-114

Calculatus Eliminatus 36, 63
Carroll, Lewis 10-11, 15†24, 19†30, 126
Cat in the Hat 36, 63-64
catena 12, 19
CDC 160 96-97
CDC 6400 97, 101
cell 14, 23, 29, 33-35, 39-40, 55†65, 126
character iii-iv, vi, viii, 4, 6, 8-21, 23-24, 28, 32, 35, 41-52, 55-56, 58, 60, 62, 64, 66-67, 69-70, 74-75, 81-93, 96, 100, 102, 104, 106-108, 110-111, 114-118, 120-125
cheir 12
chemical 13-14, 24-25, 39-40
chemist 24, 28-29
chemistry 6, 12, 24-25, 28, 32-33, 35, 38†58, 102, 111, 127
Chesterton, G. K. v, 4-6, 9-10, 17, 27, 30†46, 63-64, 81†71, 96, 110, 126-127
chiral 11-12, 14-15
chromosome 38
CIF iii, 37, 68, 74-75, 78-79, 110, 115, 121-123
closure 2-3, 22
codon 38-41, 112
commutative 21, 46
COMPASS 100
complete inverted file iii, 37, 68, 74-75, 78-79, 110, 115, 121-123
composing stick 13
concatenation 12, 15, 19-24, 49, 106
Consolation of Philosophy 126
conspici quam prodesse 27†40
Cray, Seymour 96†75
cysteine 112
cytosine 24, 39, 55, 111

data structure 68, 74, 115, 126-127
DAWG iii, 74-77, 115, 120
degenerate 38-40, 44
deoxyribonucleic acid vii, 3, 5, 13-14, 23-25, 31-32, 35, 38-40, 42, 44, 55, 57, 69, 81, 92, 111
deoxyribose 13, 24
Desulfomonile tiedjei 32
dexter 12
dextrose 12
Dickens, Charles 126
digit 6-7, 10
dihydrouradine 55†65
directed acyclic word graph iii, 74-77, 115, 120
dis legomena 37
DNA vii, 3, 5, 13-14, 23-25, 31-32, 35, 38-40, 42, 44, 55, 57, 69, 81, 92, 111
doctrinal principles of the thirteenth century 30†46
Drosophila melanogaster 13

E. coli 13, 30, 33†52, 35†55
Egyptian 11, 14, 98†78, 126
eigen 44

eigen-inclusion-set 50
eigencharacter 44, 46, 48-49, 55, 111
eigenstring 49-50, 72, 74
Eikenella corrodens 81
electrophoresis 25
empty string 21-23
Escherichia coli 13, 30, 33†52, 35†55
esse 12†19
Euclid 17, 126

fabula 15†24
FEL 30†46, 96-97, 99
fingerprints 33-34, 63
finite state 81-82, 84, 88
fluorescent 33-34
font 8, 13, 20†31
FORTRAN 97
Frankel Engineering Labs 30†46, 96-97, 99
Frankel, Samuel R. ii, 30-31, 96-97, 99

gallium 6
Gardiner, Sir Alan 11, 126
Gaskell, Philip 13†20, 126
gene synthesizer 33-34
glutamic acid 112
glutamine 112
glycine 112
glyph 8
Goodwin, William 8†12, 126
grammar 8†12, 11, 126
Greece vi, 8-12, 16, 18†29, 37, 98†78, 126-127
Greek vi, 8-12, 16, 18†29, 37, 98†78, 126-127
group 13, 21†32, 23†33, 29†43, 34-37, 39-40, 62, 64-66, 68-69, 73, 99-100, 111
group signature 36-37, 65, 69
groupoid 2
guanine 24, 40, 55, 111
Gulden, Samuel L. ii

handedness 11-12, 14-15
hapax legomena 36-37, 63
Hasse diagram 51-52, 57, 60
hieroglyphics 11, 14, 98†78
histidine 112
Holmes, Sherlock v
Homer 37
Homo sapiens 13, 25
HP 2116 97
HP 3000 97
Hugh of St. Victor 127
hybridize 33-35, 39
hydrolytic deamination 55†65
hypercube 57, 60

idempotent 46, 69
identity 3, 21-23, 46, 63
Iliad 37
in-situ 33-35, 39
infinity 22-23
inosine 40-41, 55†65
integer 2, 18, 22-23, 55-56, 67, 70, 82, 84-85, 88-92, 100, 102, 106-108, 115-117, 119-120, 122, 124-125
interstellar flight 60†67
inverse 21, 23, 60
iota 17
isoleucine 112
isotope 25

Jaki, Stanley L. 8†11, 126

jot 17
Juster, Norton vi-vii, 126

Kathryn Mary, Sister ii
keto groups 111
Kleene closure 22
KMP iii, 31-32, 48, 80-88, 91-92
Knuth, Donald iii, 31-32, 48, 80-88, 91-92, 126

laevus 12
lattice 47
lazy evaluation 30†46
letter vi, 3-5, 7-15, 18-22, 24-25, 31-32, 55, 60, 68, 76, 103-104, 110-112, 126
leucine 112
levulose 12
Liddell 10†15, 127
locus classicus 19†30
logic viii, 9
Lord's Prayer 16, 127
lysine 112

Mantinbrand, James H. 127
Marietti, Peter 16†25, 127
match 32-34, 36, 40-42, 44, 47-48, 50-52, 54, 58-59, 62, 67, 69, 81-83, 85-88, 90, 93
Mathemagician, The vi-vii
matrix 23†34
melting point 64
messenger RNA 35, 40-41
methionine 112
Miescher, Friedrich 23
Miller, Chris ii, 81†72
Milo vii†4
molecular biology iii, vii, 12-13, 23-25, 29†43, 36-37, 42, 44, 55, 111
monoid iii, vi, 1, 3, 14, 17, 21†32, 23
monomer 24
mRNA 35, 40-41
multiplicity 49-51, 58

National Institute of Health 27
Newman, John Henry vii, 28†42, 127
Nierzwicki-Bauer, Sandra ii, 28
NIH 27
nitrogen 23, 55
nucleic acid 23, 111†87, 127
nuclein 23
nucleotide 31, 38-40, 55, 111
null-match 43-44, 46-48, 92

Odyssey 37
oligonucleotide 39†62, 126
omni-match 43, 46, 48, 51-52, 56, 60, 111
oncogene 27
operating system 97
oro 12†19
oxygen 6, 23, 55

p53 27
Paolini, Eugene ii
paper vii, 7, 17†28, 28, 38†58, 64, 76, 114-115
papyrus 7
partial order 46-47
Pascal's triangle 62
Pascal, Blaise 62
PATRICIA 74†70
PCR 38†58
permutation 106, 108-109
Phantom Tollbooth vi-vii, 126

phenylalanine 112
philosophy v, 17†27, 110, 126
phosphodiester bond 24
picogram 38†58
polarized light 12†18
polymer 24
Polymerase Chain Reaction 38†58
pre-rRNA 39
prokaryotes 30
proline 112
protein 14, 24, 40
pseudouradine 55†65
purine 41, 111
pursos 37
pyrimidine 41, 111

radioactive 25, 33-34
radioisotope 34
radium v
Rawn, J. David 23†35, 33†52, 35†55, 55†65, 112, 127
reflexive 44-46, 48
regular expression 88†74
regular grammar 88†74
reliefpfeiler 12†19
reverse engineering 97
ribonucleic acid ii, vii, 13-14, 23-24, 30, 32-36, 38, 40, 42, 44, 55, 64, 69, 111
ribose 13, 24
Ribosomal Database Project 29
ribosomal RNA ii, 29-31, 33-35, 37-39, 64, 66, 81, 126
ribosome 14, 29, 33-35, 40
RNA ii, vii, 13-14, 23-24, 30, 32-36, 38, 40, 42, 44, 55, 64, 69, 111
Romano, Dr. Joseph ii, 27
ROMATIBISUBITOMOTIBUSIBITAMOR 12†19
Rome 8-9, 12†19, 17, 127
rRNA ii, 29-31, 33-35, 37-39, 64, 66, 81, 126

Saccharomyces cerevisiae 13
Scrabble 12, 18, 22
secondary structure 30†47
semigroup 3, 42
Semitic 8
sequence vii, 3-6, 8-9, 19, 21, 24-25, 29-35, 38-40, 44, 49, 55-56, 63-66, 81, 101, 108, 110-111, 127
serine 112
signature iii, 33, 35-37, 63-67, 69, 71-72, 75, 79, 81, 110, 125
SINUMMIIMMUNIS 12†19
sodium cyanate 24†36
sodium hydroxide 28
spacer 39
star-closure vi, 22, 49
stereochemistry 12†18
stereoisomer 12†18
string iii, vi-vii, 4-6, 10, 12-24, 31-33, 35-37, 40, 42, 44, 48-52, 54, 58, 60, 63-72, 74-76, 78-92, 94-95, 98, 100-110, 115-116, 119, 125
Svedbergs 35†55
symmetric 11, 44, 48

tartaric acid 12†18
taxonomy 39†60
thirteenth century 27, 30†46
threonine 112
thymine 24, 55, 111
tittle 17
transfer RNA 13†20, 35, 40-41, 55†65

transitive 44-46, 48-50, 81, 86-87
trie 74†70
tRNA 13†20, 35, 40-41, 55†65
tryptophan 112
typesetting 13, 20
tyrosine 112

uracil 24, 55†65, 111
urea 24†36

valine 112
venae comites 4†6

Waclawik, James M. ii, iv
Ward, Maisie 4, 126-127
water 24†36, 28
Watson, John H. v
Watson-Crick 12†19, 40, 55-56, 69†69
Widor, Charles 31
wildcard iii, vii, 23, 25-27, 32, 35-52, 55-57, 60, 62, 64-65, 67-68, 71-72, 74, 80-89, 91-93, 111-112
wobble base 38, 40-41, 112
word ii-iii, vi-viii, 3-7, 9, 11-16, 18-19, 22, 24, 28†42, 30, 37, 46, 48, 74, 76, 96, 110, 126
Wöhler, Friedrich 24†36

Zea mays 13

* * *

Made in the USA
Middletown, DE
03 July 2024

56779210R00080